To Mary McCartan
with all good
wishes
Alfred D Kelley
7-30-77

by

Alfred D. Kelly

DORRANCE & COMPANY

Philadelphia

CONTENTS

Chapter

I

EARLY DAYS IN THE LAW DEPARTMENT

When I first joined the Law Department of The Delaware and Hudson Railroad in 1918, Mr. Lewis E. Carr was counsel in charge. Mr. Carr was one of the outstanding lawyers of his day and was held in great esteem by both bench and bar.

Near the close of Mr. Carr's career, when he was close to eighty, I recall going with him to the Appellate Division of Supreme Court in Albany, where he argued the appeal of a railroad negligence case. In the course of his argument that day Mr. Carr started to read from his brief—something the Supreme Court of the United States had said in a similar case—when he was kindly interrupted by Mr. Justice VanKirk, presiding, who said: "Mr. Carr, you won't have to read that, we'll read your brief." Mr. Carr calmly removed his glasses. looked the judges over deliberately and replied: "If you do that, all right."

The judges enjoyed a hearty laugh. They got the sly implication that perhaps lawyers' briefs are not always read as avidly as zealous advocates hope they might be.

* * * * *

On another occasion as we walked up State Street hill on our way to the New York Court of Appeals, I mentioned to Mr. Carr the fine rapport he seemed to enjoy with the judges of all of the higher courts. He said, "Well, that's true, I guess. Although I have perhaps vexed and annoyed them at times, they have for the most part remained my friends—at least it seems that way. The only exception I can recall was Judge Haight of our Court of Appeals. A few years ago I lost an important case where the court divided in its decision four to three against me. Judge Haight was one of the four judges supporting the prevailing opinion. I felt very strongly that the decision was wrong and applied for reargument of the appeal, which was granted. On reargument I cited, and stressed rather vigorously, a previous decision of the court in a similar case in which Judge Haight had written the opinion, and which seemed to me to be directly contrary to their conclusion in my case. Before I could complete my argument, Judge Haight picked up his papers and walked out on me. The same thing happened on my next two appearances before the court, so I made it my business to call on His Honor in chambers. After a somewhat strained discussion of the incident, the judge accepted my assurances that no personal affront was intended, that perhaps I was carried away in my zeal, etc. We shook hands, had dinner together at the Fort Orange Club and when Judge Haight retired I was gratified when asked to deliver the principal address of the evening at his retirement dinner."

Mr. Carr finished this interesting story just as we climbed the steps of Court of Appeals hall. I never did think to ask him how he made out on the reargument of his appeal that brought about the whole misunderstanding.

* * * * *

I recall Mr. Carr relating that many years ago he was in Saratoga Springs, in the office of Senator Edgar T. Brackett, an eminent lawyer of that era. The office looked out on Broadway. Having finished the business at hand, these two old friends were visiting and discussing, of all things, "lawyers." Senator Brackett said: "Lewis, there is a brilliant young lawyer coming along in this town who is likely to give you railroad people fits in the negligence field; he's going places."

Just then Mr. Carr, looking out the window said: "Hello, someone must be hurt, there goes the ambulance," and Senator Brackett, responding excitedly, said, "Yes, and by gracious there goes that young lawyer I've been telling you about," pointing to a young man pedaling furiously on a bicycle directly behind the horse-drawn ambulance.

* * * * *

2

For several years (1914-18), following enactment of Workmen's Compensation Laws by the various states, claims and other matters pertaining thereto were handled by our Accounting Department. In 1918 management made such matters the responsibility of the Law Department and all records and personnel were transferred to that office. This was where they belonged in the first place.

Mr. W. E. Eppler, who headed the Accounting Department at the time, was unhappy over this, regarding it as a curtailment of his authority. Now, Mr. Eppler was generally able to have his own way about such things and was considered somewhat of a tiger in his *modus operandi*. He attempted to retain "a piece of the action" by writing Mr. Carr a letter in which he said that "when Workmen's Compensation claims are settled all files shall be sent to me and retained in my department."

Shortly after receiving this letter, Mr. Carr, with a twinkle in his eye, said, "Let's go down to the second floor and we'll beard the lion in his den."

As we were announced and entered "the lion's den," Mr. Eppler shook hands cordially and bid us be seated. I sat down but Mr. Carr remained standing and said, "No, this will take only a minute. It's in regard to your letter to the effect that all files in Workmen's Compensation cases, when claims are settled, be sent to your department."

Mr. Eppler said, "Oh yes, Mr. Carr, I wrote that letter."

Mr. Carr said, "Well, we won't do that!" Without another word he turned, opened the door and walked out. Need I say that ended the matter?

* * * * *

My regard for the memory of Mr. Lewis E. Carr, as a great lawyer and a person of remarkable strength of character, impels me to state a few simple facts regarding this extraordinary gentleman.

He was a most imposing figure, tall, gaunt—in the Lincoln mold—with high cheek bones, deep-set, penetrating eyes, straight

Delaware & Hudson Railway Co. General Office
Building, Albany, New York.

4

black hair and flowing mustache that showed only faint traces of grey even at an advanced age.

Habitually he wore a black cutaway coat with trousers to match and a black bow string tie. His boots were black, of fine quality, of the pull-on type with elastic sides.

He sat and worked for hours on end at a huge flat-top desk, engulfed in an array of files, letters, blueprints and legal tomes, leaving only a reasonably clear space in front of him.

All of his briefs were written in longhand on legal, lined yellow sheets, with a remarkable minimum of changes, corrections or interlineations, a tribute to his clearness of thought and grasp of the facts and applicable law.

He used ten-inch-long black pen holders, with gold points that were half the size of a man's thumb. Letters were dictated to his personal secretary, but he wanted no part of electric gadgets or "call buttons"—had them removed (when put in for him by management) upon returning to his desk after a few days in Washington to argue a case in the Supreme Court of the United States. "When I want someone, I'll walk out and ask him to come in," he said.

He smoked a huge, curved rosewood pipe, with a bowl that would accommodate about half a tin of tobacco.

When we expressed our surprise and gratitude upon being presented with a crisp ten-dollar note at Christmas time (a most generous gift in those days) he would reply, "that makes it all the more gratifying," or an equally appropriate gracious remark.

Our library was most complete and up to date. He never turned a law book salesman away without a chance to display and discuss the works he had to offer. If Mr. Carr, after listening patiently, said "no," the salesman better believe that the sales pitch was ended. If he purchased, he might, with tongue in cheek, inform the salesman that he had all the free, complementary embossed copies of the Constitution of the United States that he needed. "Just send the books, please."

Lawyers representing claimants and litigants against the railroad were also listened to with patience and courtesy. When Mr.

Carr thought they had talked long enough as to the merits of their clients' cases, he was wont to gently interrupt and quaintly ask, "What is it you wish that I should do?" If the case was one that could be settled out of court, this inquiry usually resulted in a discussion leading to a fair and reasonable settlement.

The legal briefs of Lewis E. Carr were masterpieces of logic and literary perfection, invariably supported by cases of persuasive legal precedent. Blessed with a deep, resonant voice, he spoke rapidly, distinctly and to the point. He abhorred repetition, for which the judges always appeared grateful. The many cases in which he was involved as counsel would make an imposing volume of *causes célèbres.*

An unusual case that attracted widespread attention in the early part of the century was the charge of bribery directed against New York State Senator J. P. Allds, who was tried on the charge before his fellow members of the Senate in the year 1910.

Lewis E. Carr was engaged and appeared as chief counsel for Allds, who was accused by a fellow senator, one Conger, as having, in the year 1901, while a state assemblyman, accepted a bribe of $6,000 to influence proposed legislation in behalf of a bridge building company engaged in and seeking business in the State of New York.

The following is an excerpt from part of the concluding address by Mr. Carr to members of the Senate in behalf of Senator Allds, on March 22, 1910, at the conclusion of several days of sensational testimony by witnesses for both the accuser and the accused.

I called to your attention at the outset, that he (Allds) is presumed to be innocent and must be proven to be guilty, and that where there is an explanation consistent with innocence, that is to be adopted, rather than the one consistent with guilt. What must be the answer upon the evidence here? That is the question submitted to you.

And now, gentlemen of the Senate, I come to the close of my part of this debate, and must leave the fate and fortunes of the man for whom I plead in your hands. The matter so intrusted to you is of the highest importance to the State and of the gravest consequences to him. The dignity and honor of the Senate is involved, for if the accusation made against him is proven to be true, he is no longer fit to continue a member of this body, and should go hence stripped of his official belongings and dignity, to be for the remaining years of his life a wanderer upon the face of the earth, shunned and scorned by men. You should be watchful and vigilant in your investigation into and consideration of the matters here presented. But your zeal and alertness to guard and protect the honor of the body you constitute should not blind your eyes to his rights or to the consequences to him of what you do; nor lead you for a single instant from the path along which you must travel to reach a conclusion that will be just to him as well as to yourselves. You are not here to search for and, if possible, find some one to throw overboard in the hope thereby that the waves of an angry sea may be stilled, or another near at hand to be tossed out in the expectation that by such means the appetites of those who clamor for a victim may be appeased. But you are here to search for and to find the truth, guided and governed by such rules and principles for the redress of human wrongs and the protection of human rights as since the reign of law began have proven to be efficacious and adequate to that end.

Despite Mr. Carr's able defense and strong plea in Allds's behalf, he was convicted on the charge by the Senate and resigned from that body in March of 1910. He died on September 12, 1923.

* * * * *

If I may regress for a moment and be permitted a bit of personal reminiscence, after several years in the Accounting

Department of the Delaware and Hudson Railroad, in 1918 I transferred to the Law Department as a claim agent.

After I was there a short time, with Mr. Carr's approval, I commenced the study of law, which you could do at the time by filing a law student's qualifying certificate with the New York Court of Appeals. A couple of years later, at Mr. Carr's suggestion, I enrolled as a student at Albany Law School, continuing my employment with the Law Department after school hours and evenings. Following graduation and admission to the bar in 1923, I was given an attorney's assignment with the company.

An interesting and somewhat embarrassing experience during my last few months in law school arose out of the following circumstances. Law school graduation was scheduled for June, but by reason of my clerkship study in Mr. Carr's office and my attendance at law school, I had sufficient time to my credit to, with Dean Fiero's approval and permission, take the March state bar examinations and, being fortunate enough to pass, was admitted at the May 1923 Term of the Appellate Division of Supreme Court.

I mention this not by way of suggestion of accomplishment but rather to point up an amusing aspect of the situation I found myself in for a few weeks as a full-fledged attorney at law, yet still having to pass law school examinations and to graduate. This was not made any easier by "my pals," who were quick on the draw with some good-natured "raspberries" when, all too frequently, I had the misfortune not to come up with the right answer to a question in class on torts or evidence. Naturally, I was much relieved when the hurdles of law school examinations were negotiated and commencement exercises behind me.

I still have a sneaking suspicion that the members of the class of 1923 voted me "Permanent President" for no other reason than to assuage my wounds and perhaps with some feeling of remorse for having given "the old boy" the business so unmercifully.

*   *   *   *   *

The Author—Vintage 1923

During law school attendance, writing the Ben Pitman system of shorthand, I took down and later transcribed on typewriter, most of the more important law lectures, as well as, during a short leave of absence, much of a bar examination refresher course, given by the Honorable Harold R. Medina, then an outstanding Manhattan practicing attorney and law professor at Columbia University. Later Mr. Medina became a celebrated and exceptionally able judge of the U. S. Circuit Court of Appeals.

These notes, when bound in black buckram with appropriate gold-lettered titles, such as Evidence, Negligence, Negotiable Instruments, Decedents' Estates, etc., made a useful galaxy of ready reference books. However, word got around about them and students wishing to brush up for bar examinations on particular subjects would, from time to time, borrow various volumes. Gradually they all disappeared, never to return.

*　*　*　*　*

My first appearance in Supreme Court was one not to be forgotten. This was nothing more important than appearance on Calendar Call, which ordinarily requires no great skill or preparation. Mr. Carr said, "Ask the court to have the *Harris* case go over the term, because Mr. Dugan, who is to try the case for the railroad, is engaged in a trial in Columbia County." This sounded like a simple enough assignment, and normally would have been, had I but realized that I was about run up against that distinguished jurist, the Honorable Gilbert D. B. Hasbrouck, an austere judge of experience and ability but a holy terror if he thought counsel was attempting to impede the expeditious administration of justice, as I promptly learned. When our case was called, the attorney for the plaintiff announced "ready for trial"; then I started to say, "If your honor please, the defendant would like this case to go over the term——" I got no further! His Honor interrupted to say, "Is there any reason why the plaintiff should not take an inquest (the procedure leading to a summary judgment by default)?" After a long embarrassing pause, I recovered from my surprise and managed to state the reason for our request, to which His Honor dourly listened with his usual inscrutability, to be followed by a laconic, but welcome, judicial pronouncement of "Over, next case."

I returned to the office to casually report that I had "succeeded" in getting the case over the term.

* * * * *

In my early days of incubation as a junior attorney in the Law Department of the railroad, I was frequently assigned to assist more experienced counsel in the trial of law suits against the company. Most of the cases in the capitol city of Albany were defended by Mr. Patrick C. Dugan, an able and exacting trial lawyer. Eventually I learned to work harmoniously with Mr. Dugan, but my first experience was a rather trying one.

When Mr. Dugan finished cross-examination of the first witness, he turned to me and asked, "Is there anything you think I should ask him?" Surprised but flattered, I suggested some long-forgotten foolish question. With a horrified look, Mr. Dugan whispered, "Good heavens, lad, do you want to ruin our whole case with a question like that?" I crawled back into the woodwork and when "P. C." (which I was later privileged to call him) concluded with the next witness, to my surprise he asked me the same question. Figuring I had learned my lesson, and now playing it close to the vest, I said, "No, sir," whereupon Mr. Dugan said, "Well, this is the time to speak up. It will be too late when we are back at the office." Hmmm.

A number of years later I was having lunch with Mr. Earl Barkhuff, longtime associate and law partner of the late Patrick C. Dugan. I related to him my foregoing experience. He laughed and said, "I too once suffered the same indignity. That was 'standard procedure'—his way of teaching young legal beavers humility." As Jack Benny might say, "We-l-l...."

* * * * *

11

Another early experience that taught me a lesson was a motion by the railroad for a change of place of trial for the convenience of witnesses, before Judge John Alexander at a Special Term of Supreme Court. Opposing the motion for the plaintiff was the late James A. Leary of Saratoga Springs, an experienced and highly successful negligence lawyer. After listening to arguments pro and con, his honor interrupted my discourse to say, "Motion granted." However, in my zeal, I continued on with the idea of completing my argument on the particular point, whereupon Judge Alexander, with a full calendar ahead of him, interrupted with a terse "I said your motion is granted, counsellor." With that we took our departure.

On the way out of the courthouse Mr. Leary had this bit of sage advice. "Listen, any time a judge says 'motion granted' stop right there, pack your papers and get out fast. I learned long ago that if you insist on prolonging the argument you may well persuade His Honor to change his mind."

Henceforth, Special Term motion proceedings found me ever "at the ready" for a fast take-off in the event of a favorable pronouncement from the bench.

* * * * *

An illustration of Mr. Dugan's resourcefulness and quick thinking was a grade crossing case growing out of a collision between a train and an automobile. A very near-sighted civil engineer witness for the railroad was giving formal "sight distance" testimony, which ordinarily goes unchallenged, but this time, plaintiff's attorney, noticing the difficulty the witness was having reading his field notes through his thick-lens eye glasses, said: "I object to the testimony of this witness. It's obvious that he is not a person of normal vision and therefore wholly unqualified to testify as to the distance an approaching train could be observed from the highway." This didn't bother Mr. Dugan in the least. He said, "Why, that's all right, your honor; a man of normal vision could probably have seen this train twice as far." Judge Ellis J. Staley, Sr., presiding, never did get to rule on the objection and it was passed over by everyone with a good-natured laugh.

*   *   *   *   *

Another crossing case that comes to mind that produced some bizarre developments was a case where a truck driver was struck by a passenger train. He claimed that the crossing watchman was slow in getting out on the crossing and did not give adequate warning of the trains approach. In a pre-trial conference in our office, Mr. Dugan noticed one prospective witness, a squat Italian with one short leg, walking about with a slow-motion, dipping gait. He asked, "Who's that fellow?" When told that was our crossing man, he said: "Good heavens, if the jury sees him walking around like that, they will certainly say that he could not get out on the crossing in time." He then said: "Tell that fellow when he's called in court to come up as fast as he can." Perhaps I briefed him too well. When called, he leaped from his seat in the rear of the courtroom and bounded up the aisle like a scalded kangaroo, ending up in a flying leap into the witness chair. Everybody gaped in amazement.

He was finally put under oath at the direction of Judge Hasbrouck, presiding, and Mr. Dugan, through an interpreter, because the man could speak little English, adroitly proceeded to establish that the watchman was out on the crossing, with stop sign in hand, *in advance* of the train's approach. He then asked him, "Now, as plaintiff in his truck approached the crossing, what if anything did you do?" The witness jabbered heatedly back and forth in Italian with the interpreter and when the latter hesitated Judge Hasbrouck impatiently looked over his glasses and said, "Well, come, come my man, what does he say?" Whereupon the interpreter blurted out, "He says 'I yelled go back, you son of a (censored).'"

In his charge to the jury Judge Hasbrouck said, "I am constrained to recognize that the crossing watchman, in spite of his obvious infirmity, can indeed move with alacrity in extremus. His lexicon of appropriate expletives also appears adequate.

However, in arriving at a verdict, you shall disregard the use of anathema by the crossing man and my commentary in regard thereto as having no relation whatsoever to the merits of the case."

* * * * *

One of the really great trial lawyers in our Third Judicial District of Supreme Court in the early nineteen hundreds was the late Abbott H. Jones of Troy, New York. For a number of years, following my admission to the bar in 1923, it was my privilege to be frequently associated with Mr. Jones in the defense of law suits against the railroad in Rensselaer County.

One of Abbott's most formidable adversaries in the negligence field was the late Tom Powers, also of Troy. When these two bitter rivals locked horns, sparks were sure to fly.

I recall one occasion, to show his complete disdain for Mr. Powers, when it was the latter's turn to address the jury in a negligence action against the railroad in the county of Rensselaer, Jones promptly arose and quietly left the court room. After a few sulfurous blasts calculated to show his contempt for Mr. Jones, Powers turned and discovered to his dismay that his hated rival had thought so little of what he had to say that he had left the court room. Powers was so furious and upset that his argument to the jury became quite disjointed and apparently ineffectual. The jury's unanimous verdict was a no cause of action.

As we took our departure I said, "Abbott, your leaving the court room during Mr. Powers's address, if designed to upset him, certainly seemed to have the desired effect, but wasn't that a pretty risky thing to do not to be there and hear what Tom was saying?"

Abbott replied, "Don't worry, I didn't miss a thing. You know, that mahogany partition back of the judge's rostrum extends only part way to the ceiling. I left by the side door, cut through the lawyers' room and from the corridor back of the partition heard about every word he said."

15

Only then did I realize that Jones in his address to the jury had indeed countered—with, shall we say, appropriate retaliatory derision—most of the points Powers had made during Jones's "absence." It became obvious that the cagey Mr. Jones had missed little of what the frustrated Mr. Powers had told the jury.

Jones's friends in the Troy area were legion. Opposing lawyers were on occasion disposed to lament the difficulty in finding jurors who had not at some time or other been helped or befriended by Abbott Jones, who evidently had faith in Shakespeare's admonition about keeping one's friendship in repair.

To be sure, lawsuits should be determined on the evidence rather than on friendship. But I have yet to hear a lawyer gainsay the comfort of a friendly jury.

*　*　*　*　*

A number of years ago our company was sued, and successfully defended, in multiple actions in Supreme Court at Troy, claims of navigation companies that the railroad was guilty of negligence and nuisance in reconstructing its railroad bridge over the Hudson River in that city and was responsible for alleged money damages of over $600,000. It was contended that during a severe late spring freshet in the river, the railroad caused damage to equipment (tugs and barges) and delay and loss of profits in reaching destination at various Great Lakes ports by reason of obstructions which narrowed the navigable channel under the bridge.

The fact that the railroad, prior to the trial of these civil actions, had been indicted in Federal Court, on complaint of the United States Corps of Engineers, for failure to promptly remove the alleged obstructions in the river, as demanded, did not tend to improve the image or posture of the defendant railroad on the trial of these civil actions, even though the indictment had been conditionally dismissed prior to the trial.

Once again we could be thankful for having the professional talents of Mr. Abbott Jones as counsel in that case. He selected the jury and did most of the cross-examination of witnesses.

It was claimed by the plaintiffs that the only place at which difficulty was experienced in navigating at the time was at or in the immediate vicinity of defendant's bridge and that they had no trouble in proceeding up the Hudson River from New York City until they reached Troy. It was decided to subpoena the *log books* of the various tugs and barges and this was done. A quick examination of these books and records gave the lie to the claim of "No difficulty" in navigating south of Troy and the information in the skillful hands of Mr. Jones proved quite devastating on cross-examination. The following brief excerpts from the record of the trial are illuminating:

The witness Fred W. Clark, captain of the plaintiff's tug *Pearl Harbor,* after describing the difficulty in effecting passage at the bridge at Troy and stating that he observed nothing unusual about the water on the way north, testified as follows to Mr. Jones's questions:

Q. "What did you stop at Coeymans for?"
A. "To single the tows out."

Q. "For what purpose?"
A. "To make them easier in towing."

Q. "Well was it because of the very high water in the river that that was necessary?"
A. "No, sir."

Q. "That was not necessary?"
A. "No, sir."

Q. "What do you mean by making them tow easier?"
A. "If you single them out you would not have so much water to break."

Q. "Now you came all the way from New York to Coeymans without breaking it up?"
A. "Yes, sir."

Q. "I notice in your log here you say that you are 'hanging on' at Coeymans on May 12th. What did you mean by that?"
A. "Make fast to the pier."

Q. "Was it the high water that required you to hang on, as you say, at Coeymans?"
A. "No, sir."

Q. "Is this your log book that I show you and is that your handwriting?"
A. "Yes, sir."

Q. "Will you read the third line for the jury?"
A. "Hanging on at Coeymans...."
Mr. Jones: "Go ahead, read the rest of it."
"...on account of high water."

Q. "Was that the reason you landed there?"
A. "We had orders to land there."

The witness Mortimer W. Dolloff, captain of the plaintiff's tug *Holbrook*, admitted reluctantly, when confronted with his log book notations, that the barges he had in tow had been swept up on the "flats" at Coxsackie south of Albany due to the flood and currents. He then testified as follows, on cross-examination:

Q. "Did you notice anything unusual about the conditions of the river on your way up?"
A. "Why, not to any great extent."

Q. "Then why did you enter upon your record on May 17th, while you were at Coxsackie, 'water high and running wild?'"
A. "Why, I believe I made a note of that."

Q. "And you do say it was running wild?"
A. "It was in certain spots, yes."

Q. "And when you made the record of the water running wild, did you mean it was just a little high water?"
A. "Why, I meant there was high water in places. You take any creek or anything with a little high water, it will run faster in the narrow places."

Q. "Well, up here at this bridge at Troy, it is narrow too, is it not?"
A. "Yes, sir."

Joseph McCormack, a fleet captain for the plaintiff, acknowledged that under normal conditions they made the trip from New York to Troy in from thirty to forty-eight hours. At the time in question he admitted it took nine days to get there.

There was much other testimony along the same line. The jury's verdict was a unanimous no cause of action. However, Judge Hasbrouck, presiding, set the verdict aside as "against the weight of evidence" and granted a new trial.

This now put the railroad in the position of having to appeal the Hasbrouck determination to the Appellate Division of Supreme Court. Just about this time, Judge N. P. Willis, counsel for the railroad at Albany, died suddenly. Pending appointment of a successor for Judge Willis, Mr. H. T. Newcomb, who at the time was our General Counsel in New York City, would come to Albany once a week to sort of "keep an experienced eye" on things.

Mr. Newcomb was an outstanding "big city" corporation lawyer of distinguished mien and possessor of an extensive vocabulary. On his first visit to Albany, following Judge Willis's untimely passing, he asked me what I thought should be done about perfecting our appeal and preparation of a brief. I told him I had taken it upon myself to prepare a brief and had a rough draft of a typewritten manuscript on my desk. The preparation of this brief, I might say, after a week of trial, many witnesses and much conflicting testimony, was not an easy task and I had spent considerable time in research on the law and examination of court decisions in similar cases.

Mr. Newcomb seemed surprised, and perhaps pleased, that the matter had not been allowed to slumber. He said, "I'll take the brief and let you have my comments and suggestions." As he arose to leave he said, "Be kind enough to keep me currently advised of all significant developments." With that, he straightened the ribbon on his pince nez, adjusted his Madison Avenue Homburg to the proper angle, picked up his chamois gloves and cane and strode from the room, headed for a waiting taxi and the railroad station. About a week later Mr. Newcomb told me he liked the brief and was having it printed in New York. (I still have a yellowed, faded copy in my personal file at home.)

If I may be pardoned a personal note, following our success on appeal to the Appellate Division (the Court reversed Judge Hasbrouck's decision and reinstated the "no cause" verdict of the jury, thus terminating the litigation in favor of the railroad), a situation arose that required me to make an important decision pertaining to my future with the corporation. I received a telephone call from Mr. Newcomb, saying he would like me to meet him at the Willard Hotel in Washington two days hence for, as he put it, "a discussion of something I have in mind."

I arrived at the hotel about 8:00 A.M. Following breakfast and a general discussion of pending matters in our Albany office, Mr. Newcomb offered me a place on his staff in New York at a substantial increase in salary. He said, "Take a week to think it over and 'phone me next Tuesday morning."

At the time we had two small boys and were in the process of planning a new home in Loudonville. After much thought and discussion with Mrs. Kelly, I decided to remain with the company at Albany. It was not an easy decision to make.

Many years later, on January 1, 1961, to be exact, I retired from the service of the railroad. I would have to say that these were most enjoyable and rewarding years, especially in the matter of valued, lasting friendships and, I like to feel, perhaps of useful accomplishment.

* * * * *

II

OTHER COURT AND RELATED INCIDENTS

Following Mr. Carr as counsel for the railroad was the late N. P. Willis, a former county judge from Cooperstown. Judge Willis had a rather surprising experience in the trial of a railroad negligence case in his home town, where he was very popular. In examining a prospective Supreme Court juror, plaintiff's attorney asked him if he knew Judge Willis. When he said that he did, he was asked, "How well?" and the fellow said, "Sometimes when I meet him on the street he will say 'hello' and sometimes he won't." Now Judge Willis was not about to let the jury panel get the idea that he had gone "high hat," so when it came his turn to examine this prospective juror he reminded him that he suffered from narrow vision and consequently did sometimes, unintentionally, pass people he knew on the street without speaking. To everyone's surprise the fellow said, "Aw that's o.k., judge, I just wanted to get on the jury so that I could help you out." He didn't make it!

* * * * *

Speaking of the selection of jurors, the story is told about the trouble the lawyers on both sides had in a case in upstate New York in examining an intemperate female juror.

The attorney for the defendant said: "Do you know the lawyer for the plaintiff?"

She answered, "I do, and he's the biggest crook in the state."

The attorney for the plaintiff then stood up and asked, "And do you know my opponent, the lawyer who just questioned you?"

She nodded, "Yes, I do, and he's a bigger crook than you are."

At this point the judge loudly gaveled for order, hastily beckoned the lawyers to the bench and whispered, "If either one of you asks her if she knows me, I'll hold you in contempt of court."

*   *   *   *   *

Another case in Supreme Court in Cooperstown that had its amusing aspects involved a collision between a train and an automobile on a local crossing. At a pre-trial conference the night before trial, with all prospective railroad witnesses present, we ran into difficulty with the old crossing watchman, who insisted that the train involved was a passenger train, although the train crew and everyone else knew it was a freight train. No amount of discussion could dissuade him or "refresh his recollection," so, not without misgivings, on the trial we simply asked if he remembered "the train involved in the accident," without reference to freight or passenger. He said that he did, so after a few other pertinent questions, followed by brief perfunctory inquiries by opposing counsel, he was permitted to step down.

We breathed a sigh of relief, feeling that any embarrassing "conflict of testimony" had been avoided. However, as the old man passed the jury box he stopped and, waving his cane dramatically, boomed: "I ain't as young as I used to be, but let me tell you that none of them law fellers can pull the wool over my eyes." Judge and jury are probably still wondering what the old gentleman was talking about.

*   *   *   *   *

A number of years ago, while awaiting our turn on argument of an appeal in the Appellate Division of Supreme Court at Albany, an amusing incident cropped up in the case preceding ours.

A north country lawyer was earnestly arguing his appeal when he was suddenly interrupted by Mr. Justice John M. Kellogg, noted for his predilection to break in abruptly on argument with a pointed question.

His honor asked, "Counsellor, was not this same case previously before this court?" When informed by counsel that it had been, Judge Kellogg inquired, "What did we decide?" The harried attorney, throwing his hands in the air in a gesture of abject despair, cried "God only knows!"

* * * * *

Occasionally even brilliant judges will forget momentarily that they once practiced law themselves.

Perhaps one such occasion was the time a young lawyer, limited by the Court to only thirty minutes for his oral argument, had no more than started to plead his cause when he was interruped by former Associate Justice of the Supreme Court of the United States, Felix Frankfurter. Frankfurter was relentless with his questions. With time running out, this can, of course, be a nerve-wracking experience for the attorney.

After ten of his allotted thirty minutes had been used, the lawyer looked up helplessly and said: "Mr. Justice, I would love to answer all of your questions, but I would also like to point out that time passes ever so much more quickly on my side of the bench than yours."

* * * * *

Following Judge Willis's sudden and untimely passing, about 1927, Judge Joseph Rosch left the New York Supreme Court bench to become counsel for the railroad at Albany.

Judge Rosch, after a most successful career as a general practitioner and trial lawyer in Sullivan County, was elected to the Supreme Court bench in the Third Judicial District of New York while still a comparatively young man. One of Judge Rosch's favorite stories had to do with his first appearance as a Supreme Court Justice in Rensselaer County.

When he arrived at the court house in Troy the day before the opening of the term he found his court room crowded, having been taken over by the county judge for the trial of a murder case. Elbowing his way through the standees near the door, he asked a crusty court attendant how much longer the criminal case on trial would likely take. With a withering look the attendant said: "You drop back tomorrow morning, boy, and I'll let you know."

Judge Rosch politely said, "Very well, I'll be here," and took his departure.

Next morning, with litigants, lawyers, prospective jurors, *et al.*, assembled, the court crier intoned the traditional "Hear ye, hear ye, the Honorable Justice Joseph Rosch, presiding . . . . " The door from chambers opened and the judge, in full court attire, ascended the rostrum and assumed his place on the bench. Judge Rosch related with a smile that out of the corner of his eye he spotted the court attendant in question, who suddenly seemed to look quite ill as he attempted to busy himself to avoid His Honor's deliberate mischievous glance. Judge Rosch said that for the remainder of the term the poor, unhappy man always seemed to be busy with a pole adjusting windows and shades whenever he happened to glance in his direction.

Judge Rosch and I spent more than thirty years in association in the Law Department. Those were most congenial and pleasant years.

* * * * *

A number of years ago when we had the steam locomotives, a train jumped the track one night in the city of Saratoga Springs and the locomotive "telescoped" an adjacent store and dwelling. One of our trainmen and his wife lived upstairs over the store. He filed a claim and after we settled with him for a reasonable sum, someone said: "Mr. Johnson, that must have been a terrifying experience. What did you think when it happened?"

He said: "Well, sir, when the crash came the wife and I were in bed. I was thrown out on the floor. Beams were creaking, plaster was falling, the room was filled with steam and the noise was terrific, but I kept my head. Jumping to my feet, I said to my wife, "Mary, you better get up now, I think something's happened!"

This will have to go down in history, I believe, as one of the greatest understatements since Noah said he thought it looked like rain.

* * * * *

The late Honorable O. Byron Brewster, New York Supreme Court Justice, and a resident of the lovely county seat village of Elizabethtown in the northern Adirondacks, had a raft of "mountain folklore" stories that he loved to tell when court would adjourn for the day and bench and bar would move "with all deliberate speed" to the Windsor Grill or the lounge of the Deer's Head Tavern, there to indulge in a bit of convivial libation, to be regaled by His Honor's matchless wit and to bask in the warmth of his genial charm.

One of his favorite stories, that seemed to defy authentication, was about the village handyman, a well-liked character, who when he died and no relatives could be found, was buried by his friends and honored by the town by being "laid out" in the fire house. One of the court attendants at the time, although usually on the job by day, managed to get stoned regularly by night, so some of the village jokers moved the corpse to his favorite pub and propped the body against the bar. When the court attendant came in, already "smashed," he lunged up to the bar and slapped the corpse on the back, inviting him to have a drink. As the body fell to the floor, the conspirators ran out of hiding yelling, "Why did you kill him?" to which the drunk responded defiantly, "Why, he pulled a knife on me."

* * * * *

A story that has been going the rounds for a long time in the north country also concerns Judge Brewster. As the story goes, an important law suit came up for trial before the judge and a distinguished metropolitan lawyer was engaged to assist local counsel in the case. On the opening of the trial, apparently seeking to flatter His Honor, the visiting attorney referred to the beauty of the Adirondacks, its lakes and streams and said what an honor he considered it to be to be able to try the case before a judge so eminently qualified to hear and decide the issues, etc.

26

"MARY, YOU BETTER GET UP NOW, I THINK
SOMETHING'S HAPPENED!"

At this point a local loud-mouthed character in the rear of the court room, apparently unimpressed, yelled, "Oh, Bosh!"

As the fellow was ejected, the lawyer, now quite upset, approached the bench and said that he hoped the court would agree that the remark was uncalled for and ill-timed. His Honor replied: "I quite agree that the remark was indeed uncalled for and ill-timed, and I hope for the remainder of the trial no one will shout 'Oh Bosh' until they have heard both sides."

* * * * *

Another popular and able judge was the late Earl H. Gallup. Term after term for many years he was returned to office by an admiring electrorate as Albany County Judge.

As a member of Wolfert's Roost Country Club I was frequently a playing partner of Judge Gallup. He was an excellent golfer—when he could keep his cool.

In court and about town he was a compendium of decorum, calm, affable, unruffled. However, he never quite accepted the axiom that "golf is a humbling game." There was nothing humble about His Honor's approach to golf. A tall, handsome, powerful man, he played the game with a grim, frightening determination. As he took his cut at the ball or made his putt, players and caddies stood transfixed, holding their breath. It was said that even birds in the trees feared to chirp.

On one terrible day the judge drew a caddy suffering from a bad cold. On several occasions His Honor blew his top when he flubbed his shot as the caddy sneezed at the top of the judge's back swing.

The fifteenth hole at the Wolfert's Roost Club is a tricky par 3 with a large pond directly in front of the tee. On the sad day in question His Honor plunked his ball into the pond, then threw his club in after it. When it looked as though the ailing caddy was about to suffer a similar fate, the judge's playing partners quickly surrounded him and one fellow said: "Please, judge, take it easy. The caddy didn't sneeze that time."

Jumping up and down in his fury His Honor yelled, "I know he didn't, but I allowed for it."

* * * * *

On another occasion after a bad golf shot Judge Gallup hurled his offending five iron a record distance into the forbidding forest bordering the seventh fairway. After a futile five-minute search for the club by foursome and caddies, the judge's caddy called out, "I'm afraid we can't find it, judge." From the abysmal depths of the jungle, the judge's voice rang out, "Never mind the club, find me."

* * * * *

A prisoner serving a long sentence for armed robbery at Clinton State Prison, wrote an appealing letter to Judge Gallup, who had sentenced this man. He said it was a matter of great personal importance that he talk with the judge. Judge Gallup agreed to see the man and made the long journey from Albany to Dannemora.

As the judge stood with the warden, watching the men return to their cell blocks after outdoors recreation, Judge Gallup was surprised by the number of prisoners who recognized him. Some shook hands, others said, "How are ya, judge?" or, in jest, "What are you in for, judge?" etc.

As the last of the convicts passed, Judge Gallup turned to the warden, shook his head sadly and commented, "My alumni."

* * * * *

At a reception honoring the judges of one of our appellate courts, one judge, when offered a drink, graciously accepted, then remarked: "You know, I never refused a drink in my life except once, and that was when I misunderstood the question."

* * * * *

This brings to mind the story told about President Harry Truman, when offered a drink at a morning Washington wedding reception. Declining the offer, he said, "Thank you, but I never take a drink before noon time." Then, before the party making the offer could get too far away, the President said, "On second thought, I'll take that drink—it must be noon time somewhere."

* * * * *

Thomas Leaming, in his book *A Philadelphia Lawyer in the London Courts* (Holt & Co., 1911), attributes the expression "a case for a Philadelphia lawyer," to a case that arose in Albany, New York, in 1734. The unpopular royal judges of the Province of New York, it is related, indicted a newspaper publisher for libel in criticising the court and they threatened to disbar any lawyer of the Province who might venture to defend him. An old Philadelphia lawyer, a former student of the English Inns of Court, made the long journey to Albany and by his skill and vehemence, actually procured a verdict of acquittal from the jury under the very noses of the obnoxious court. The fame of this achievement spread throughout not only the colonies but the mother-country itself.

* * * * *

The story is told of an upstate Justice of the Supreme Court who was temporarily assigned to hold a term of court in New York City. On the opening of the term, with the large court room well populated by lawyers having business before the court, proceedings were interrupted by the siren of a passing ambulance. As the sound faded in the distance, His Honor remarked (with a straight face and tongue in cheek) that he wanted to congratulate the lawyers present for their admirable restraint and self-control as it was his observation that not a single member of the bar left the court room.

* * * * *

At one time and for a great many years the Delaware and Hudson Railroad, through subsidiary companies, operated a fleet of palatial and beautifully maintained passenger steamers on Lake Champlain and Lake George. The general manager was a doughty gentleman by the name of Daniel Loomis of Burlington, Vermont. On a bright sunny day in August, 1927, as the steamer *Sagamore* pulled away from the old Marion House dock on Lake George, due to improper blocking, a beautiful new Cadillac motor car, owned by a Mr. Sidney Cohen, president of the Motion Picture Theatre Owners of America, rolled overboard and sank in thirty feet of water. After several days' effort the automobile was recovered and, after being dried out and having a new battery installed, was driven under its own power about seventy miles to a Cadillac agency in Albany, where it was, despite such performance, declared "dead on arrival." I recall going out to Richfield Springs, where Mr. Cohen's lawyer was summering, and settling his claim for market value of car and contents.

Mr. Loomis then found himself stuck with a soggy, water-logged Cadillac that no one would buy, so being the resourceful gent that he was, he wrote the president of Cadillac, told him the story of the "remarkable comeback" of this automobile after recovery from the bottom of Lake George and offered him "a good deal" on this car, which he thought would be invaluable for advertising purposes to show how a Caddy could take it. He received a courteous reply, but no deal. The letter ended something like this: "We appreciate your offer, but frankly this is nothing unusual for Cadillac ... just another illustration as to why Cadillac is recognized as the 'STANDARD OF THE WORLD.'"

Mr. Loomis's only comment? "Well, I tried!"

* * * * *

31

A somewhat less humorous incident, at about the same time, involved boat line operations on Lake George. This had to do with the playing of music for dining and dancing by an orchestra of young college musicians aboard the steamer *Mohican.* An enjoyable time was being had by all nightly to the strains of the latest tunes of the day when, 'by the light of the silvery moon," the leader of the band and the Lake George Steamboat Company were served with summonses and complaints alleging violation of a federal statute governing the playing publicly of copyrighted music.*

There undoubtedly having been violations of the law, (the party doing the hiring is equally guilty under the statute), there was nothing else to do but plead guilty to the charge, pay the fine and necessary fees and go on about our business, much the wiser for the experience.

* * * * *

In a case tried in Supreme Court, Albany, before the late Honorable Kenneth S. MacAffer, the plaintiff, a fast-talking female, sued her hostess by reason of injuries claimed to have been sustained as the result of a fall in the latter's bathroom. With the plaintiff on the witness stand, veteran court reporter Bill Craft complained that he could not keep up with her. Judge MacAffer asked, "How far did you get?" and Craft said, "She lost me in the bathroom." Turning to the witness Judge MacAffer said: "Repeat the last part of your testimony, madam, and when you come out of the bathroom, please bring Mr. Craft with you."

* * * * *

*The statute in question was passed by Congress during the Theodore Roosevelt administration, at the behest of the late great composer, Victor Herbert. It is policed and enforced by the American Society of Composers, Authors and Publishers (ASCAP). They fix the fees and keep a wary eye out for violators.

The late P. J. Tierney of Plattsburgh, New York, was for many years one of the outstanding "north country" trial lawyers. He was frequently called upon by our company to serve as counsel in important litigation against the railroad in Clinton and Essex counties. Near the end of his career, "P. J.," as he was affectionately known, was beginning to suffer from loss of hearing. On the trial of one of our cases, a local lawyer, in no way involved in the case and, in a not too ethical gesture, offered this "free advice" to Mr. Tierney's adversary: "Keep your voice down when examing witnesses and you can get away with murder on Pat." The recipient of this intelligence, a lawyer of integrity and a good friend of P. J's, informed the latter during lunch of the advice he had received. Mr. Tierney went down the street, purchased a hearing aid and, returning to the court room, immediately ran into "Mr. Busybody," who said, "Well, P. J., I see you have a hearing aid," to which Mr. T. responded, "Yes, and you know something, I find it works very well on voices pitched deliberately low."

Following the foregoing incident, Mr. Tierney, now completely sold on the value of a hearing aid, kept urging a friend and fellow lawyer who was having difficulty to get one. At long last his friend agreed to give it a try.

Shortly thereafter Pat met his friend on the steps of the courthouse and observed, "Well, Tom, I'm glad to see you have finally gotten a hearing aid."

"Yes," said Tom, "and I'm delighted—should have taken your advice long ago. I can hear everything now, one hundred percent."

"Great," said Pat, "what kind is it?"

Glancing quickly at his watch, Tom replied, "It's a quarter to two."

* * * * *

Judge James Gibson, a distinguished member of New York State's highest court, the Court of Appeals, tells an amusing story of a lawyer who was said to have had too many double martinis during lunch. This left him in a rather ugly mood for an afternoon court appearance, and he had the effrontery to tell the judge that he was stupid. The judge said, "You're drunk, sir."

The lawyer replied, "I know it, but tomorrow I'll be sober but you will still be stupid."

* * * * *

A lawyer was reading to relatives the will of a wealthy client. After reading several substantial specific bequests, he came to the name of a not too favorite nephew of the testator. The lawyer read, " 'And to my nephew whom I promised to remember, Hi, Charlie.' "

* * * * *

At a well attended social gathering a lady who had a sore throat asked a doctor guest if he would look at her throat. Although annoyed by the request, the doctor did so and when the lady moved out of earshot, the doctor turned to a lawyer he knew, standing nearby, and asked him whether he thought he should send the lady a bill. "By all means," advised the lawyer.

The doctor thereupon in due course sent the lady a bill for $25.00 for professional services. Shortly thereafter the doctor received a bill from the lawyer for $25.00 for legal advice.

* * * * *

Honorable Fred A. Young, presiding judge of the New York State Court of Claims, former Republican state chairman and former state senator, is a tremendously popular gentleman with a great sense of humor.

Among many honors received, Judge Young was once made a Knight of the Order of Merit of the Republic of Italy and given a citation by the president of Italy.

Back at his office an aide, upon examining the citation, said, "Why, judge, did you know that under this citation you are now entitled to be called 'doctor'?"

"Okay," the judge replied, "but don't get sick."

* * * * *

A cross-eyed city traffic court judge, upon taking his place on the bench one morning, found three traffic violators standing before him. The judge looked at the man on the right and said, "What's your name?"

The man in the middle said, "Sam Hayes."

The judge glared at him and said, "I wasn't asking you. Please remain quiet until I speak to you."

And the man on the left said, "I didn't say a word, Your Honor."

* * * * *

An escaped prisoner, upon being recaptured, was brought before a southern judge and charged not only with unlawful flight but also with the theft of a prison uniform. The judge threw out the theft charge, ruling that it was unreasonable to expect the prisoner to run about town in his shorts.

* * * * *

A lawyer at the conclusion of a successful trial of a case in behalf of his client said to the latter: "Here's my bill. You can pay $300 now and $100 a month for the next three years.

"That sounds like buying a car" said the client.

"I am," said the lawyer.

* * * * *

An amusing incident we once overheard in Supreme Court was this: The attorney in an automobile case was attempting to discredit a witness with respect to his ability to judge distance. The following questions and answers are informative.

Q. "How long would you say this court room is?"
A. "52 feet 6 1/2 inches."

Q. "What makes you so certain and precise?"
A. "Well, I once served on a jury and I heard you ask a guy that same question, so I thought I better measure it."

* * * * *

In a case tried in Scranton, Pennsylvania, against the railroad, where the plaintiff was seriously injured as the result of a collision between a train and an automobile, it was claimed that the watchman did not lower the gates in time. Right up to the time of trial he insisted he had put the gates down in ample time, but during the trial of the action he broke down on cross-examination and gave this excuse for his dereliction of duty: "Lately I have been attending a series of revival meetings in my church, and having gotten religion, at the time of the accident I was in my cabin reading my Bible and praying."

His Honor observed: "Ah, you did not read your Bible correctly. If you had done so you would have seen that your Bible says, 'Watch and Pray'—now you did not watch."

* * * * *

Mr. Paul Bedford, outstanding lawyer, philanthropist and prominent citizen of Wilkes-Barre, Pennsylvania, whose law firm represented the Delaware and Hudson and its subsidiary coal mining properties for many years, tells this amusing incident of his only journey into politics. Many years ago, as a young up-and-coming attorney, he was persuaded to run for a seat on the city council. Near the close of the voting day (by ballot in those days) his precinct received a 'phone call from the all-powerful local Democratic leader, who wanted to know how Bedford was doing in the voting. When informed that it looked "very close," the "boss" bellowed, "Well, dammit, how many votes does he need?"

* * * * *

A prominent attorney, with a lucrative practice, that we have known for many years, tells this amusing story. His father had retired as chief of police in their town. He had become quite bored with retirement so his son gave the old gentleman the job of keeping his law library picked up, the books in place, etc., and each Friday gave him a check for his services. Coming to the office early on a Monday morning, the lawyer was surprised to find his father seated at his desk with the latter's checkbook spread out in front of him. The old man asked: "Did I get my pay check last week?"

His son said, "Why sure, Dad, last Friday as usual. But may I ask what you are doing with my checkbook?"

Whereupon the old gentleman arose and with great dignity replied, "That, sir, is none of your business!"

* * * * *

Let's not overlook that legendary railroad case, generally attributed to the Lackawanna Railroad. The attorney for the railroad was pleased when the crossing watchman withstood a vigorous cross-examination with his testimony unshaken that he was indeed out in his proper place on the crossing with lantern in hand. However, the watchman confided to his conferees, after the jury had brought in a verdict in favor of the railroad, that "I'm sure glad no one thought to ask me whether or not my lantern was lighted."

* * * * *

The Honorable James McPhillips of Glens Falls, a distinguished citizen of that lovely vacation area of New York State and a highly respected justice of the Supreme Court, told me this story about a justice of the peace, who was not a lawyer, in one of the small communities in Washington County. Two country lawyers were having at it before the old justice in a breach of contract case. His Honor seemed to favor the contention of the defendant. The plaintiff's lawyer then flashed an opinion of a five-judge appellate court, which he contended was "on all fours" with the claim of his client, although it appeared that the court had divided three to two. The Justice said, "Let me see that

37

case." After reading and puzzling over it for some time he finally said brightly, "Ah you think that case was three to two in your favor, but that ain't so at all, because it says two of the judges *concurred*, which of course means that they *conquered* the judge who did the writing. That really made it four to one against. O.K.?"

* * * * *

A farmer sued the railroad for loss of his cow when it was struck by a train of the defendant. On the trial his attorney asked the farmer these questions and received the following replies:

Q. "What was the first thing you saw?"
A. "I saw the cow coming out of the alfalfa."

Q. "Then what happened?"
A. "I saw the alfalfa coming out of the cow."

* * * * *

A prominent judge of Children's Court in a large city, unwilling to accept the claim that the juveniles of today are any worse than those of yesteryear, has the following stinging sentences framed over his desk with the footnote indicated:

Our youth now love luxury. They have bad manners, contempt for authority, disrespect for older people. Children nowadays are tyrants. They no longer rise when their elders enter the room. They contradict their parents, chatter before company, gobble their food and tyrannize their teachers.

Note: The writer? Socrates. The time? The 5th Century before Christ.

* * * * *

Lord Coleridge, a famous English advocate, and later Chief Judge of England, on a stop-over visit in Chicago was approached by a gentleman of the press who said, "I guess the conflagration we had in this little village of Chicago must have made your great fire of London look pretty small," to which Lord Coleridge blandly responded, "Sir, I have every reason to believe that the great fire of London was quite as great as the people at that time desired."

* * * * *

A famous lawyer, orator and great wit was the late Honorable Joseph H. Choate, former ambassador to England. He died in 1917 at the age of eighty-five. Many of his *bons mots* and witty sallies are legendary, particularly those pertaining to his practice of law, both in and out of court:

One day a pompous young man came into Choate's office and though the lawyer was busy demanded to see him immediately. "Take a chair," said Choate, quietly, still working.

"But I am Bishop So-and-so's son," declared the young man.

"All right," patiently replied Choate, still continuing his work, "take two chairs."

* * * * *

On another occasion a clergyman, protesting Choate's bill for services in settlement of a large estate, said, "I always understood that you gentlemen of the bar were not in the habit of charging clergymen for your services."

Choate replied: "You are in error. You clergymen look for your reward in the next world, but we lawyers have to get ours in this."

* * * * *

During the trial of an important law suit, after several tiffs with the court, when Choate turned his back for a moment the judge became infuriated. "Mr. Choate," he asked, "are you trying to show contempt for this court?"

"No, Your Honor," replied Choate quickly, "I am trying to conceal it."

* * * * *

A number of wealthy residents who owned mansions in the Stockbridge and Lenox area of Massachusetts, including Mr. Choate, had formed a cemetery association. A number of their loved ones had been buried in the plot acquired.

Some of the members of the association felt the cemetery property should be fenced. When Choate, who was also attorney for the association, was approached for his opinion on the matter, he expressed the view that a fence was unnecessary. "Those who are in," he said, "can't get out, and those who are out have no desire to get in."*

* * * * *

An old English Lord Chancellor, when asked how he made his selection from the ranks of the barristers when obliged to name a new judge answered: "I always appoint a gentleman, and if he knows a little law so much the better."

* * * * *

Lord Alverstone, chief judge of England (1900-13), in his "Recollections of Bar and Bench," tells an amusing incident that occurred in an English Court in the City of London. A celebrated lawyer by the name of Joseph Brown was arguing a case before Chief Justice Jarvis—a man of very acute mind and a rapid

* The Choate anecdotes are reprinted from Cleveland Amory, *The Last Resorts*, Harper & Row, Publishers.

thinker. Brown, who could never be made to hurry, was proceeding with his usual caution when the chief justice impatiently interrupted him: "Get on, Mr. Brown, get on."

Brown stopped and said: "I beg your Lordship's pardon, but I apprehend that my argument cannot proceed with as much rapidity as your lordship's mind."

"For God's sake, don't stop to tell me that," moaned the chief justice.

*　*　*　*　*

The late Judge Hiscock of our New York Court of Appeals could, when he felt the occasion required, embellish a sentence in a most picturesque manner.

I recall a matrimonial case, the result apparently of a hasty and imprudent marriage, that came before the court. Because of the prominence socially of the litigants the case attracted more than passing interest.

Judge Hiscock wrote the opinion for the seven-judge court, in the course of which he said: "Before cohabitation had increased the undesirable possibility of their foolish misadventure, they parted." (Like in "Lucky they had not kids," one might say.)

*　*　*　*　*

The late Dean J. Newton Fiero, Albany Law School, addressing a first day freshman class some fifty years ago said:

As a matter of historical interest you are today commencing the study of law in a building that was once an abandoned gas factory.

We do not regard this as an insurmountable obstacle to eventual success at the bar. As a matter of fact, some of our distinguished alumnae are inclined to look back upon it as more or less of an inspirational asset.

41

I hasten to add that Albany Law School, Union University, is now quartered in one of the most beautiful and functional buildings of its kind in the United States.

*　*　*　*　*

On another occasion, a student quizzed by the Dean as to certain recent court decisions ("required reading"), and having displayed a woeful lack of familiarity therewith, desparately volunteered, in extenuation, that he was well versed on the statutes. This prompted the following bit of biting raillery on the part of Dean Fiero: "Young man! Do you realize that you may one day wake up to discover that some legislature has repealed your brains?"

*　*　*　*　*

Plaintiff, claiming permanent injury—complete paralysis from the waist down—as the result of the alleged negligence of defendant motorist, sued and obtained a verdict of $300,000 in a Supreme Court civil action, although there was evidence indicating that said injuries might not be as "permanent" nor as serious as claimed.

A furious claim investigator who had worked on the case for the insurance company said to the plaintiff as he was wheeled from the court room on a stretcher, "We will follow you for the rest of your life and the very first time you put your feet to the ground to walk you'll be jailed for your fraud and deception."

The fellow said: "O.K., but I'm on my way now to take a jet plane to Paris, and from there I'm going to the shrine at Lourdes, and, brother, you're about to witness one of the greatest miracles of all time."

*　*　*　*　*

In a divorce case, in a state recognizing "cruel and inhuman treatment" as grounds for relief, among other specific allegations of the complaint was one to the effect that on a certain date

42

Albany Law School, Union University, Albany, New York.

the defendant had thrown and struck the plaintiff with a heavily bound book, cutting her on the head. On the trial, when asked for an explanation of this incident, the defendant explained: "Well, it was this way. We had a few cross words. I was reading this book and turning the pages when suddenly it flew right out of my hand."

Counsel for the plaintiff caustically observed, "From a circulating library, no doubt."

* * * * *

A wealthy Jewish gentleman approached his lawyer and longtime friend and said he wanted to revise his will and wished his attorney to make all final arrangements, in advance, for his funeral. The lawyer said, "O.K., Jake but where would you like to be buried, Forest Lawn, Gates of Heaven or Memory Gardens?"

Jake said, "Surprise me."

* * * * *

In a case on appeal in England a prominent English barrister, irked by an expression by one of the judges about his opinion as to the law of the case, remarked petulantly: "If that's the law, my Lord, I'm burning my law books in the morning," to which his honor tartly replied, "I suggest you might better consider reading them."

* * * * *

A lawyer I know tells this story. Whether fact or fiction I'm not sure. He claims he called a plumber to open a kitchen drain. When the man finished, the lawyer asked, "What do I owe you?"

The plumber said, "Well, let's see; I supplied no parts or materials, so that will be just 1 1/2 hours labor at $26.00 an hour, or a total of $39.00."

The lawyer said, "Why that's outrageous. I never made that

kind of money practicing law," and the plumber replied, "I never did either when I practiced law."

$$* \quad * \quad * \quad * \quad *$$

A veteran attorney was asked by a young lawyer if he still found practicing law as much fun as it used to be, and he replied: "Look, son, at my age nothing is as much fun as it used to be."

$$* \quad * \quad * \quad * \quad *$$

A woman who claimed to have witnessed an accident, a "hit and run" matter, from her front window when a twelve-year-old boy was struck by a truck, was called as a witness on the trial of the action in Supreme Court, Rensselaer County. When asked whether she could identify the driver of the truck in court, she said "Yes, that's him right over there," pointing to the number four juror.

$$* \quad * \quad * \quad * \quad *$$

The courts of the Emerald Isle, both past and present, are rich in legal lore and humor.

History records that in the early nineteenth century there was little love lost between the aristocratic English judges assigned to the tight little isle and the patriotic Irish barristers. There were many stinging exchanges and displays of wit between bench and bar. For example:

A courageous and witty Irish advocate was the honorable John Philpot Curran. After several cutting remarks in Judge Robinson's court, his Lordship shouted: "If you say another word I shall commit you," to which Curran replied: "If you do, we shall both have the conclusion of reflecting that I am not the worst thing that your Lordship has committed."

$$* \quad * \quad * \quad * \quad *$$

On another occasion, as Curran was addressing a jury, a jackass brayed loudly outside the courtroom window. Lord Clair, the lord high chancellor of Ireland, presiding, raised his hand and said politely: "One at a time, Mr. Curran, one at a time."

However, shortly thereafter, it was Curran's turn. As Lord Clair was summing up for the jury, he paused for a moment and at that instant the same jackass brayed again, whereupon Curran remarked in a stage whisper, "Hasn't this courtroom a remarkable echo?"

* * * * *

Once Lord Clair brought a large dog into the court room. As Curran earnestly argued an important point of law, his lordship showed his contempt by scratching the dog's head and leaning over to whisper to it, making it perfectly clear that he was paying no attention to Curran's argument. Suddenly Curran stopped speaking and when Lord Clair looked up and asked, "Why have you stopped, Mr. Curran?" the latter replied smoothly, "I am sorry, but I thought your lordships were in consultation."

* * * * *

Exchanges of this kind are perhaps now a thing of the past in the court rooms of Ireland, although there is still humor of another sort.

Thus, an elderly man from the mountains, who had sustained serious injuries in a motor car accident and was suing for damages, was present at a pre-trial court room consultation at which a physician displayed X-ray plates of the plaintiff's head and traced the fine line of a skull fracture. The man was much impressed by this proof of his injury, and as the actual trial was about to start and the parties concerned took their places before the bench, he called out in a loud whisper: "For Heaven's sake, doctor, don't lose that map of me head."

* * * * *

Today, when suddenly everyone appears to be ecology-minded, it is interesting to note the apparent failure of the courts and public, early in the nineteenth century, to recognize the seriousness of the environmental problem. This is well illustrated in the following English case of *Res v. Medley*, (6 Carr. & Payne 292):

In that case, the defendant Medley was indicted "for conveying into the river (Thames) the refuse of gas, whereby the water was rendered unfit for drinking, the fish were destroyed and fisherman damaged in their calling."

With the indifference apparently characteristic of the times, the Court said: "If the diminution of fish is to be considered the criterion, then every proprietor of a copper-bottomed vessel, every maker of a sewer, every proprietor of a steamboat must be found guilty***." The Court went on to say that if the people wanted their conveniences (sewers and the like) "they must be content to bear the inconvenience which will occasionally result from the use of them."

* * * * *

In a case reported in England a number of years ago, a plaintiff sued a property owner for damages for killing his dog. A sign on the property read "all dogs found on these grounds without their owner will be shot."

The Court instructed the jury that they should find for the plaintiff because it must be presumed that dogs can't read.

* * * * *

In another British case a man sued a property owner and recovered a substantial verdict by reason of having been bitten by the owner's dog, although a sign said "Beware of the Dog." In that case it was proven that the plaintiff couldn't read.

The Court suggested that the property owner, instead of a printed sign, should have had one that showed a picture of a dog taking the seat of a man's pants. This, he thought, would be adequate warning to those who could read as well as to those who could not.

* * * * *

In another English case involving ownership of a dog, the judge directed that the dog be brought into Court for a "recognition test." When the test proved inconclusive, the dog displaying equal affection for both claimants, one man said he was sure the dog was his because, when he sniffed the dog all over, "The odor was unmistakable."

The lawyer for the other side then said he felt that this test had also to be considered inconclusive unless the claimant could pass a similar test with the dog doing the sniffing.

* * * * *

Another amusing English case of many years ago (not of the "doggy" variety) was a case where the judge expressed his personal view in a negligence case to the effect that a traveler who is injured "as a member of society ought to bear his breaks and bruises uncomplainingly, as part of the unavoidable ills that society is heir to."

Counsel for the plaintiff cryptically replied: "I suggest, my Lord, that every man ought to be left to his own taste in this respect."

* * * * *

It is refreshing to note that the House of Lords, that august deliberative and debating body of Merry Old England, can afford the world a delightful chuckle or two from time to time, in spite of such difficult and important problems it must currently struggle with, such as a lack of industrial productivity, the housing shortage, the Common Market, juvenile unrest, etc., not to mention the diminution in importance around the world of its soccer teams.

Its titled leaders somehow manage to retain their traditional sense of humor, as displayed in the following debate recently with respect to the fundamental issue of cruelty to monsters.

What prompted the discussion was a proposal to try and determine once and for all whether or not there was indeed a Scottish Loch Ness Monster.

It appears that under an act of Parliament passed years ago half in jest, any monsters that may be present in Loch Ness are protected animals. The *World Book Encyclopedia* proposed a search of Loch Ness by a submarine, equipped to bring back a flesh sample, if possible, by means of a biopsy dart shot from an air gun. The following colloquy is illuminating:

Lord Kilmany (to Lord Hughes, Joint Parlimentary Under Secretary of State for Scotland): "Is the noble Lord aware that the Chief Constable has given permission for an attempt to be made to obtain a tissue sample from whatever monsters can be found?"

Lord Hughes: "My Lords, the organizer has said that the main objective of the submarine will be to try to get a positive identification of any echo which may be picked up by sonar equipment. For this purpose, it will be fitted with arc lights and photographic gear.

In addition, it will have a small compressed air gun, designed to fire a retrievable dart, so shaped as to extract a small sample of tissue for subsequent analysis. This technique is widely used for tagging whales. In the particular context of this scientific expedition, I hardly think it constitutes damage or assault."

Lord Hawke (now taking up the cudgels): "My Lords, how would the noble Lord like to be 'potted' by an air gun to take samples of his tissue?"

Lord Hughes turned the question aside urbanely. "My Lords, provided that the relevant part of my tissue was no greater than the small amount, in proportion, that was taken from the bulk of the whale, I doubt whether I should notice it."

And there the matter appears to have rested.

* * * * *

One of the most beautiful and historical old court houses in the United States is the Colonial Court House at New Castle, Delaware. Its history dates back prior to the American Revolution.

In addition to the historical articles that have been written regarding this fine old building, there are many amusing anecdotes concerning the people connected with it in those early days. One in particular concerns a celebrated lawyer of that era named Thomas McKean, who became chief justice of the counties embodying the New Castle Judicial District.

Judge McKean, it appears, was a huge man who delighted in the formalities of office. When he sat on the bench, he wore an immense cocked hat and a brilliant scarlet gown. It is stated that one day when a mob had assembled outside the court house, Chief Justice McKean sent for the sheriff and commanded him to suppress the riot.

"I cannot do it," replied the trembling sheriff.

"Why do you not summon your posse?" thundered the scowling chief justice.

"I summoned them but they are ineffectual."

"Then, sir, why do you not summon me?"

The sheriff was stunned for a moment and then gasped out: "I do summon you, sir."

Whereupon, it is said, the large chief justice, scarlet gown cocked hat and all, swooped down from the courthouse on the mob like some gigantic avenging angel and "catching the ring leaders by their throats, he knocked their heads together, thus quelling the riot."*

* * * * *

A litigant, claiming injuries when he fell on the stairs of a

---

* This story is taken from William Prickett, *American Bar Association Journal*, November 1970, p. 1067.

mercantile building, sued and on the trial was asked by the attorney for the defendant:

Q. "At the place where you fell, as you contend, did this stairway ascend or descend?
Not to be outdone poetically (or in absurdity) he replied:
A. "From the bottom it seemed to upward wend, from the top it would tend to downward bend."

* * * * *

A will, dated April 1, 1939, which bequeathed the bulk of a large estate to a person not a blood relative of the testator, was contested by two nieces of the decedent, attacking the validity of the instrument. The case presented a good illustration of the advisability of employing expert witnesses in their field. An authority on the subject of "Fraudulent and Disputed Documents" was employed and he was able to prove that the alleged "will" was indeed a forgery. It was signed with a ball point pen *before* ball points pens had been invented. Someone suggested that the big mistake of the forger was picking out April Fools Day to date the fraudulent document.

* * * * *

In the early days of the New York State Workmen's Compensation Law, when benefits were less liberal than they are today (nothing for the first fourteen days of disability then only two-thirds of daily wages), our chief claim agent sent the following form letter to an injured employee:

Dear Mr. Houlahan:-

Beg to advise that our records indicate that having been disabled fifteen days you are entitled to one day's compensation at two-thirds of your daily rate, or a total of $9.25. Please indicate your acceptance.

The letter came back with this notation:

> Beg to advise that we don't do business that way.
> (signed) Charlie Houlahan's wife.

* * * * *

In a suit against the railroad for destruction of an automobile when struck by a train of defendant on a grade crossing, counsel for the railroad asked this question and received the following reply:

> Q. "Is it not true that when you heard the locomotive whistle around the bend you bailed out and abandoned your car on the crossing?
>
> A. "No, sir. When I heard the whistle I said to the girl friend, 'we better get out now and go for gas.' "

* * * * *

In a civil action for damages against the railroad for death of a motorist when struck by a train on a public crossing in Pennsylvania, on the trial, based upon the results of an investigation of the accident, it appeared essential for the railroad to prove that there was a violation by the decedent of the "Stop, Look and Listen" law of that state. With that in mind, the engineer of the train involved was called as a witness and after the usual preliminary questions he was asked: "As the decedent approached the crossing in his automobile what if anything did he do?" Our anticipated answer, of course, was that he continued across in front of the train without stopping, which appeared to be the fact. However, the engineer's surprising but somewhat pious answer was "he just looked up at me and smiled."

* * * * *

A law suit that produced a chuckle or two involved at the time a somewhat abrasive veteran chief engineer, who had been in the service of the railroad for a great many years. He was an individual noted for his very positive personal opinions, quick temper and gruffness with those under his command. The action arose out of a lawsuit by the city of Albany against the railroad. To improve and develop its large classification yards south of Albany the railroad obtained proper authority to fill and cover over Island Creek, a stream which cut through the railroad yard and emptied into the Hudson River, and to substitute a pipe culvert to take care of the flow. Soon after completion of the project there was trouble. Whenever there was a heavy rainstorm, dwellings, stores and other places of business were flooded in that section of the city. The municipality finally brought action against the railroad, alleging that the company had miscalculated the capacity of the stream and demanding remedial steps be taken forthwith. Following a day and a half of trial, and after a parade of witnesses voicing complaint, it began to look as though the city authorities were not too far "off the beam" in their contention, although our crusty and determined chief engineer stuck by his guns that the railroad was not at fault.

During luncheon recess we talked with our construction engineer, a capable man who had been in charge of the installation of the culvert. Out of a clear sky he said, "I told 'the Chief' I thought that pipe was not large enough."

When the chief was confronted with this bit of intelligence, he blew his top and yelled, "Get that fellow down here, I don't remember any such conversation." When the assistant came into our office the chief bellowed, "Did you tell our attorneys that you informed me that pipe was too small?"

Being the frank and honest gentleman that he was, he answered quietly, without hesitation, "Yes, sir."

The old chief, taken completely aback by this apparently unexpected candor, fumed and sputtered for a few moments, then said, lamely it seemed, "Well, if it was that important you should have put it in writing."

That afternoon, at a conference in the judge's chambers, at our request, we reached an amicable settlement with the city, both sides agreeing to share the cost of substituting a larger pipe. So ended the lawsuit and the flooding in "the south end."

* * * * *

Another law suit involving our Engineering Department that gave us some anxious moments arose out of the following circumstances:

To reach and serve new industry and to tap potential revenue-producing territory, the railroad company contracted to extend one of its branch lines an additional number of miles through rugged, mountainous terrain.

The contractor who did the work, in cooperation with our engineering forces, performed an excellent job. However, when the line neared completion the contractor found he had on hand several pieces of heavy equipment, such as power shovels, trucks, bulldozers, cranes and the like, that had taken a beating and which the contractor felt had outlived their usefulness.

He advertised for purchase bids. The successful bidder was one of many junk dealers offering to buy. He made his down payment and arranged with the railroad for delivery on his rail siding at his plant many miles away.

When the shipment arrived the junk dealer, alleging breach of contract, refused acceptance and sued the contractor and the railroad company.

What happened was this. After the sale, the contractor went to the site and directed his superintendent to demolish the equipment, stating "junk he bought and junk he gets." With the assistance and at least tacit approval of the on-the-job engineer for the railroad, they proceeded forthwith, with their joint forces, to give the machines the old "swinging iron ball demolition treatment." When the residue was loaded aboard rail gondola cars for transportation it was indeed strictly junk and no longer recognizable as anything but.

On a trial in Supreme Court the plaintiff junk dealer maintained he had purchased the equipment as is for a good and valuable consideration, in good faith, and was entitled to delivery of same in the condition which it was in at time of purchase.

The contractor contended, in which the railroad perforce concurred, that the stuff was sold for junk and at junk prices. Moreover, he testified that the equipment was "beyond reliable repair and proper functional rehabilitation."

At this juncture counsel for the plaintiff asked the witness (contractor) whether the above quoted language, indicating that the equipment was beyond repair, was his own language or that of someone else. The witness replied, "Frankly, that's 'lawyer talk'; if you want it my way I'd just say it couldn't be fixed."

The jury decided in favor of the defendants. You can be sure we breathed a sigh of relief.

* * * * *

III

PROCEEDINGS BEFORE VARIOUS
REGULATORY AGENCIES

The many proceedings that we had over the years before various state regulatory agencies, such as Public Service and Public Utilities Commissions, produced their share of amusing legal incidents:

One that comes to mind was a passenger train service case before the New York Public Service Commission. The Commission's hearing examiner, as is customary, requested that those present give their names and addresses to the hearing stenographer and state whom they represented.

A catholic priest arose, gave his name and church affiliation, then said, "I appear for the prot-est-ants"—rather than pro-test-ants.

* * * * *

When we applied to the New York Public Service Commission a number of years ago to close and discontinue our Esperance station in the Susquehanna valley and to divert the business to Delanson station, about five miles away, there was great opposition locally, principally on the ground, as claimed, that Esperance was in a "snow belt" and that the roads would be blocked and dangerous to travel a good part of the year. Our division agent was called by the railroad in rebuttal. He testified that the claim was unfounded, that the county did a fine job of plowing and sanding and keeping the highways open for traffic and travel.

When I turned the witness over to the attorney for the objectors for cross-examination, he jumped up and, shaking his finger at the witness, said: "Didn't you hear farmer Williams testify that last winter there were times when he had to hitch up his team to get his family to church?"

The witness blandly replied, "Sure, but I know lots of people that it takes a team of horses to get them to church."

*　　*　　*　　*　　*

On another occasion we were waiting our turn to be heard before the New York Public Service Commission. The case ahead of ours was a hearing on a petition by another railroad for authority to curtail certain passenger train service. There was opposition from most of the communities affected. One municipality was represented by a youthful attorney and the lawyer for the railroad, always in a jocular mood, kept referring to the young man as "my young friend Perry Mason." For example, he would say, "Now my young friend, Perry Mason, contends," etc. etc. After a while the young attorney apparently got a little tired of the Perry Mason bit, so he arose and said to the lawyer for the railroad, "If I'm Perry Mason, then you must be Hamilton Burger, that distinguished but perennial all-time loser."

Anyone who watched the old Perry Mason series on T.V. will recall that Hamilton Burger (played so well by the late William Tallman) was the "fall guy" district attorney who never won a case against Perry Mason.

*　　*　　*　　*　　*

It is now generally agreed that automatic, electrically operated short-arm gates, now in general use at railroad-highway grade crossings, afford the best protection yet devised, short of a complete separation of grades. However, the Crossing Watchmen's Union, in the interest of perpetuating jobs, almost invariably opposed railroad petitions to substitute such automatic protection for manual. This was especially so in the state of Pennsylvania. In a hearing before the Public Utility Commission at Harrisburg, in a case of this kind, the attorney for the union asked our signal engineer this question: "With a train approaching and with these short-arm gates down, would it not be possible for motorists proceeding in opposite directions to run around the gates and to collide on the crossing?"

I said: "Just a minute. The railroad will concede that such a suicidal maneuver would very likely result in a three-way tie if counsel for protestants will concede that a railroad crossing is a pretty poor place to play 'Ten Little Indians.'"

The presiding commissioner looked thoughtful for a moment, then said: "I think I shall take judicial notice of the calamitous consequences that would appear to be inevitable under such a devious misadventure."

This bit of forensic grandiosity brought puzzled expressions to the faces of most of us present and when someone of lesser pedantic erudition, perhaps, said, "How's that again?" the commissioner with a frown and some display of annoyance replied, "In simple language, what I was trying to say was that I thought that would be a hell of a good way to get killed."

* * * * *

An interesting although hardly amusing case we had before the New York Public Service Commission was a petition by the then State Department of Public Works to require the abandonment of a railroad underpass and the construction of a new one at a nearby location in Broome County, New York.

The state claimed this was necessary because of excessive curves in the county highway approaches to the existing underpass, "that could not be corrected," although it was admitted that the existing structure was high enough, wide enough and in good state of repair.

The problem the railroad was faced with was this: If the existing underpass could be made to adequately meet the necessities of the situation by improvement in highway approaches, there would be no need for any expense on the part of the railroad company, straightening of approach curves being the sole responsibility of the state. On the other hand, a new relocated underpass, under existing law, would require the railroad to assume one-half the cost, estimated, in total, at $200,000.

A railroad survey showed that the approach curves at the existing underpass could be corrected, entirely in keeping with state promulgated "required standards." It was also developed that in recent highway construction throughout the state, the state itself had introduced curves equal to or in excess of those proposed by the railroad at the location in question. Moreover, it was learned that the state had made a study plan, which they declined to produce, of highway approaches to the existing underpass that lent credence to the fact that elimination of excessive approach curves was entirely feasible. However, the commission's examiner denied the railroad the right to prove these things and refused to receive in evidence plans and study maps tending to sustain such a valid conclusion.

On the record, it was difficult to avoid the implication of a somewhat arbitrary determination to make the railroad company a participating party in the cost of an expensive, and, as we believed, unnecessary, new underpass structure.

Perforce we finally made what is called in law an "offer of proof"; that is to say, we offered to prove (1) That the approach curves to the existing underpass could be improved without any expense to the railroad, with much less expense to the state and still be within so-called state safety standards and (2) To show that the petitioner, the State Department of Public Works, had developed a plan (not produced) showing that approaches in the highway could be redesigned to utilize the existing underpass without sacrifice of "state standards," and (3) That granting of the petition in question would result in a taking of railroad property without due process of law and a gross waste of public funds.

At the conclusion of this offer of proof, the following colloquy took place:

Examiner Wilgus: "Mr. Kelly, are you not attempting to avoid my ruling by making this offer of proof?"

Mr. Kelly: "Not at all. I am simply exercising our legal right to have a complete stenographic record by asking to have marked for identification only all of those plans and other legal documents that you have refused to have marked in evidence. This, sir, is not an evasion of your ruling or a mark of disrespect. I hope there will be no occasion for an appeal to the courts from any order of the Commission, but if that should become necessary I'm sure you must appreciate what an anomalous situation would be presented if the court, on appeal, does not have before it for examination all plans, maps and other instruments that are the basic subject of controversy."

Examiner Wilgus (after off the record conference with associates): "Your offer of proof, Mr. Kelly, is denied."

From an order of the Commission, directing the closing and discontinuance of the existing underpass and the construction of a new one (with the railroad required to assume 50% of the cost) the railroad appealed to the Appellate Division of Supreme Court. The court unaminously reversed the order of the Commission, holding the action of the Commission, including its denial of the railroad's "offer of proof," to be arbitrary and capricious.

* * * * *

A number of years ago we applied to the Public Service Commission to abandon a little-used station in a small village along the shore of Lake Champlain in northern New York. In the course of the hearing one man, after stating his general objections to the proposal of the railroad, said: "There's something else that I would like to get off my chest. The railroad company moved that outdoors toilet from where it was near the station to that knoll smack dab up against my back yard fence, and"— pointing to the railroad's division agent—"the fellow that did it sits right down there in the front row. I think he did it on purpose because he doesn't like me."

Our agent jumped up and demanded to be heard, and the examiner, suppressing a smile with difficulty, said, "Very well, you may give us your version of this transplant."

Our agent then said: "It's true, we did move that toilet from where it was to where it is, back there on the knoll, but I can assure you that was not done in spite but solely for the convenience and enjoyment of patrons of the railroad. From that vantage point, with the door slightly ajar, it affords a beautiful view of Lake Champlain."

*   *   *   *   *

In another proceeding before the New York Public Service Commission, on an application by our company to discontinue poorly patronized and unprofitable passenger trains on the Cooperstown branch, a large delegation appeared at the public hearing in Albany, represented by an attorney, voicing strenuous opposition, claiming the absolute necessity of passenger train service to satisfy the transportation needs of their community.

When witness after witness admitted sheepishly on cross-examination that they had come to the hearing by automobile, although convenient train service was shown to be available, we were granted permission by the hearing examiner to ask the following general question: "How many persons appearing here in opposition came to this hearing by train?"

When not a single hand was raised, the attorney for protestants, obviously on the spot, said lamely, "It was such a nice day and the highways were in such beautiful condition that we decided to come by automobile."

The Commission granted the railroad's petition.

*   *   *   *   *

A number of years ago our road had its problems involving complaints with respect to curtailment of unprofitable passenger train service on our Ausable Branch, between the city of Plattsburg and the village of Ausable Forks, culminating in some rather hectic proceedings before the New York Public Service Commission.

Living in Ausable Forks at the time was the renowned author and artist, Rockwell Kent, famous for his painting and other works of art, his expeditions to Greenland and other parts of the world and law suits against various corporations, interestingly covered in several of Mr. Kent's books. (In more recent years there has been considerable notoriety growing out of Mr. Kent's friendship with the Soviet Union).

At the time in question, Mr. Kent returned to Plattsburg from one of his numerous journeys about the world and was chagrined to find the passenger schedule and service to Ausable Forks considerably curtailed. He promptly started a series of letters, published in the Ausable Forks newspaper, taking the railroad to task for its action. At length a local banker, who controlled the newspaper and was on the board of managers of the railroad and who was quite incensed over the criticism, instructed the editor to not publish any more of Mr. Kent's letters. When the latter learned why his caustic epistles were not being given the publicity Mr. Kent felt they deserved, well, "the fat was in the fire," as the saying goes. Mr. Kent wrote the governor complaining bitterly about "the service." Eventually the matter reached the Public Service Commission and that administrative body proceeded forthwith to hold public hearings, both in Ausable Forks and in Albany.

Feeling ran high, running the gamut from casual wrangling to vitriolic comment. At length the Commission directed restoration of service, to see whether suggestions for improvement and other "innovations" proposed would revive the dwindling patronage and declining revenues.

After about six months, when matters went from bad to worse (some trips there were no passengers; on other trips, more often than not, the number of men in the train crew exceeded the number of passengers), the railroad applied to the Commission to reopen the matter, and although there was still some opposition, particularly from Mr. Kent, the Commission finally authorized the railroad to discontinue all passenger service on the branch.

I recall during one of the early Commission proceedings in the matter at Ausable Forks, when recess was taken for lunch following a morning hearing punctuated by considerable asperity, I found myself strolling along with Mr. Kent on our way to the Village Inn dining room, when, surprisingly, Mr. Kent remarked, "You know under more favorable auspices and away from the courtroom I don't think I would find you railroaders such bad fellows after all." Hmmm.

While many perhaps may disagree with Mr. Kent's political views and ideology, no one could ever accuse Mr. Rockwell Kent of being dull.

Recently Kent's lovely home in Ausable Forks was destroyed by fire. He died in the spring of 1971 at the age of eighty-six.

* * * * *

The closing and discontinuance of poorly patronized and unprofitable railroad stations and diversion of business to adjacent other full-time agencies usually requires application to the appropriate state regulatory commission. Over a period of more than thirty years I can recall well over one hundred such proceedings by our company, necessitated by the inroads of competing forms of transportation by highway, buses, trucks and private automobiles and later compounded by airplane competition. Nevertheless, such applications were invariably vigorously opposed, more often than not by reason of "local pride" rather than because of any great inconvenience that might result.

Typical of *witness exaggeration* in such cases is the testimony of a "leading citizen," proprietor of a village store, taken verbatim from the record of a hearing in such a proceeding, with only a change of names. After testifying elaborately on direct examination as to the necessity of passenger train service and even more extravagantly as to his dependence on railroad freight service for the handling of commodities, essential in the operation of his general store, he then testified on cross-examination as follows:

Q. "Mr. Smith, when was the last time you used the passenger train service at your station?"

64

A. "Let me see, last February, I think—yes, February."

Q. "Well, this is November, how many times have you used the train service in the last ten months?"
A. "Once in January and once in February."

Q. "Do you own and operate your own automobile?"
A. "Yes."

Q. "The fact that you used the passenger service only in winter months, does that suggest to you that you patronize the service only when the weather might be unfavorable and that you prefer your own car when the weather is fair?"
A. "Sometimes I use the trains in nice weather."

Q. "When was the last time you used the trains prior to January of this year?" (long pause)

Q. "So long ago that you can't remember?"
A. "Well, I'd have to look it up."

Q. "Your store is the principal and largest store in town, is it not?"
A. "Yes."

Q. "What do you sell?"
A. "We have a large meat and grocery department, and also deal in farm supplies, feeds, general merchandise and hardware."

Q. "What would you estimate the inventory value of your stock in trade?"
A. "As of when?"

Q. "Today."
A. "Oh, at least $75,000."

Q. "In other words, you carry a large stock at all times to accommodate your many customers?"

A. "Oh yes, we have to."

Q. "Now Mr. Smith, I call your attention to the fact that railroad company's Exhibit A, shows that the only freight business Smith's store did with the railroad in the last ten months consisted of one carload of feed and four less than carload shipments, received. You shipped nothing by railroad in that period. Would the number of shipments mentioned enable you to maintain a stock in trade value of $75,000?"

A. "No."

Q. "So that you obviously receive the bulk of your goods, wares and merchandise by some means of transportation other than by railroad. Isn't that true?"

Attorney for Protestants: "Objection."

Railroad Counsel: "I'll rephrase the question."

Q. "What means of transportation, if any, other than railroad, do you employ to obtain the necessary goods, wares and merchandise for your store?"

Attorney for Protestants: "Objection."

Hearing Examiner: "Overruled. The witness will answer."

A. "Well we use the trucking lines like most everyone else because they give us door-to-door delivery."

Q. "How far is your door from the railroad station?"
A. "Oh, about a half a block, I guess."

Q. "Where do you do your banking?"
A. "Oneonta."

Q. "How far is that from your store?"
A. "Four or five miles."

Q. "How often do you go there?"
A. "About twice a week."

Q. "As you know, the railroad maintains a full-time agency station at Oneonta. Would it be any great inconvenience to pick up your occasional 'LCL' shipment at Oneonta station?"

Attorney for Protestants: "I object to the word *occasional.*"
Railroad Counsel: "All right, strike out *occasional.*"

A. "Yes, it would be inconvenient."

Q. "Even though the average this year, as shown by Exhibit A is only one less carload shipment received every ten weeks?"
A. "Next year it might be more."

Q. "Have you notified the trucking lines that you plan to return some of your business to the rails next year?"

Attorney for Protestants: "He doesn't have to notify them."
Railroad counsel: "Yes, I know that. We were just wondering what the witness had in mind when he said 'next year it might be more' and if we could look forward with a degree of hope for improvement in business at this station. I'm sorry to say I see no indication of that."

Q. "Let's face it, Mr. Smith. Isn't it true you patronize competitive highway trucking services almost to the exclusion of the use of rail facilities?"
A. "Well, I'm not going to admit that."

Q. "Would you mind repeating that last answer?"
A. "I said, 'I'm not going to admit that.'"

Q. "That's what I thought you said. Now if customers patronized your store as sparingly as you use the rail and station facilities, how long do you think you could remain in business?"

Attorney for Protestants: "Objection."
Railroad counsel: "All right, I won't press the question. We will let the record speak for itself. That's all, Mr. Smith, thank you.
"We respectfully submit, Mr. Examiner, that claims of public convenience and necessity would seem to require something more substantial than the negligible use of this station and facilities, as disclosed by the evidence."

* * * * *

An amusing incident, concerning an appeal from a decision of the New York Public Service Commission, arose out of a determination of that agency that denied, after protracted hearings, a petition of the Delaware and Hudson Railroad to discontinue, as hopelessly unprofitable, passenger train Number 68, operating between Whitehall and Albany.

This being a commuter train, there was great opposition from most of the places served. Despite the fact that it was shown the train operated at a substantial loss and that the number of passengers presenting themselves for transportation fell far short of providing reasonable financial support, the Commission denied the railroad's application and required continuance of the operation, holding that inasmuch as overall operations of the railroad, including freight, were profitable, the railroad had to "take the bitter with the sweet," as it were, in the interest of public convenience and necessity.

An appeal was taken to the Appellate Division of the Supreme Court and, based upon the record of the hearings, briefs and oral argument, the Court reversed the Commission. The decision was an important one, being, we believe, the first in which the Appellate Court had, in a passenger train service case, gone so far as to hold the determination of the Commission to be "arbitrary and capricious."

Now comes the amusing aspect of this case. Shortly after our success in the case, the general attorney for another railroad, whom I knew very well, 'phoned me to ask if I would loan him copies of all papers on the appeal in our case, particularly a copy of our petition detailing the specific allegations of error. This, of course, we were happy to do. Eventually that railroad, based upon the precedent established in our case, also succeeded in obtaining a reversal of the Commission in their case.

Some months later a large law book publishing house promulgated a series of books containing, among other things, recommended "forms" to be used on appeals from decisions of administrative agencies, taken largely from actual cases where success had crowned the effort of appellant. We considered the series a worthwhile publication and purchased the books.

When the volumes arrived, Judge Rosch, our counsel at the time, was casually thumbing through the pages of the various recommended forms when he came upon one that brought him rushing into my adjoining office, wearing a puzzled frown. He said, handing me the open book, "You know, the language of this recommended form of application on appeal in a train service case is I'm sure, the precise language of our petition on appeal in our train 68 case. But how come it's credited, word for word, to a different railroad company?"

The explanation, of course, was this: The other railroad having adopted our language in their case, and that being the latest most successful appeal, the publishing company naturally took that case as a model.

I'm afraid my distinguished colleague was more upset over the "misplaced credit" than I was.

* * * * *

69

In another New York Public Service Commission train service case, in which the Commission once again denied our petition to discontinue unprofitable operations, we applied for review of that decision to the Appellate Division of Supreme Court.

After briefs had been exchanged it became clear the Commission would have a decided edge on this appeal because of a decision of the United States Circuit Court of Appeals in a similar case that appeared to be "on all fours" with the Commission's order and determination. A careful rundown of this case in "Shepard's Citations" and other digests dashed our hope that the United States Supreme Court may have reversed the lower court, when we found no record showing that the case had gone higher.

At the time, one of our staff attorneys was a young man named John English (recently retired), who had transferred to Albany from our New York office. John was an avid reader of the court decisions as fast as they arrived in "paper back" or advance sheet form. (Judge Rosch once referred to him, in praise, as "a walking encyclopedia of cases of transcendental import.") I was lamenting to Mr. English the fact that it looked as though the Commission, in citing this case in their brief, had us over a barrel, with a case that appeared to be in complete accord with the Commission's decision. This had to be one of the luckiest conversations I ever had with Mr. English. He said, "Oh no, *that case was reversed by the Supreme Court of the United States.*"

In astonishment, I said, "Are you sure? I can find no record of it having gone further."

He said, "That's right, you won't find it in *Shepards* and the other digests. Because of certain ramifications and further activity in the lower courts, it came up again and got to the Supreme Court, but *it got there under an entirely different title.*" He thumbed through some dog-eared notes he had, ran to the law book rack and triumphantly handed me the volume he was after. Sure enough, he was absolutely right. Not only did the case go to the Supreme Court, but, believe it or not, it reversed the lower

Circuit Court of Appeals. By this fortuitous conversation we were back in business. We filed a supplemental brief and stressed the reversal, and it had to be the determining factor in the Appellate Division's reversal of the Commission's order.

A short time later, I was discussing some other matters with the Commission's counsel, Charles G. Blakeslee, in his office. Col. Blakeslee said, "By the way, how in the world did you find that strange case that got to the Supreme Court by way of the back door? We ran it down and were confident the Circuit Court of Appeals had the last word in the matter."

I said, "I didn't find it. John English of our staff found it."

Blakeslee, after a pause, said disgustedly, "Well, all that I can say is, I wish John English had stayed to hell in New York."

* * * * *

An interesting and amusing case we had before the New York Workmen's Compensation Commission involved one of our earliest claims under the then comparatively new Workmen's Compensation Law. A young man employed in our main steam locomotive shop as a helper claimed permanent damage to his eyesight from "watching a welding torch." Doctors disagreed on the question of "permanency" so pending developments he was awarded weekly compensation on a "temporary disability" basis.

When three years went by with the railroad still paying and the thing beginning to look more and more like a "life annuity," we felt some investigation was in order. Charlie, the claimant, lived on a farm, about a couple of miles from the railroad. Our Chief of Railroad Police, Joe Andres, undertook the investigation. Posing as a newspaperman on furlough because of ill health, he would call at the farm from time to time to purchase vegetables and in due course struck up an acquaintance with Charlie.

For some time there was nothing to indicate that everything was not on the up and up so far as Charlie's disability was concerned. He handled the roadside vegetable stand, wearing dark glasses and feeling his way about with a cane. However, there came a day when Andres called, but no Charlie. When informed that Charlie had taken the family "flivver" and gone into town for a haircut, our man made a beeline for the grade crossing over which the fellow would have to pass to get back to the farm. He parked his car off to one side, arranged with the crossing watchman to lower the gates as Charlie approached and made ready his trusty camera. Presently Charlie came chugging up. Down came the gates, Charlie stopped his car, a shutter clicked and Andres returned to our office, beaming like the cat that had swallowed the canary, to report his success.

A hearing was requested before the Commission, and just before our case was called Charlie, now understandably leary, arrived with his attorney. About the same time, a gentleman from the camera shop that did our developing and printing, also showed up with the telltale pictures.

When the photographs were produced it turned out they showed a pretty good picture of a well-travelled Model "T" Ford—but no Charlie! When the picture was snapped, he had dropped out of sight on the floor.

In spite of our picture snafu, as a result of Chief Andres's testimony, that of the crossing watchman who had noticed the fellow on frequent occasions driving over the crossing and Charlie's reluctant admissions under oath, we were finally able to dispose of his claim for a lump sum on a "permanent partial" disability basis.

*   *   *   *   *

Another interesting but tragic Workmen's Compensation case that comes to mind arose out of an incident in the vicinity of Plattsburg, New York.*

On a foggy early autumn morning two dangerous criminals escaped from Clinton State Prison at Dannemora and made their way southerly along the right of way of the Delaware and

* Today virtually all claims of railroad employees arising out of injuries sustained in the course of their employment are covered by the Federal Employers Liability Act.

Hudson Railroad. Surprising a track maintenance crew, they hoped aboard a rail handcar and took off, pumping furiously, pursued on foot by the railroad foreman and most of his crew. As they followed the men along the track, the crew was joined by several peace officers and an increasing number of farmers, some armed with shotguns and rifles.

Near a place called Valcour they came upon the fugitives holed up in an abandoned farm house. In a rather poorly organized approach on the criminals' "bastion," a farmer tripped and fell. As he did so, a shotgun he carried discharged, killing one of the track hands. Shortly thereafter the men gave up without resistance.

A subsequent claim to recover for the victim's death was resisted by the railroad on the ground that the accident did not arise out of or in the course of the decedent's employment, a contention that was rejected by the Workmen's Compensation Board, holding on conflicting evidence that he was directed by his foreman to join in the pursuit.

*　*　*　*　*

IV

LEGAL CONGLOMERATES

Not all legal proceedings are of the amusing variety. Quite the contrary. One of the most disturbing, sometimes disastrous, things that can happen to a lawyer in court is to be *taken by surprise* by testimony of a damaging character by one of his own witnesses while under cross-examination. At one time we had a general superintendent whom we were always reluctant to use as a witness because of his penchant to not make a complete and candid disclosure of all information he might have—*bad* as well as *good*—*before* trial. When a lawyer has full information he can often "soften the blow" and sometimes completely nullify the damaging evidence by a candid disclosure himself, certainly more melliferously than opposing counsel is certain to present it. As the saying goes, "forewarned is forearmed." I can recall one experience in particular we had with the gentleman in question. When afterwards asked why he had not told us about the matter in pre-trial conference, his answer was "I thought this was something that would hurt our case; therefore I considered it best not to mention it at all." Somehow this gentleman could not be made to understand that one should never have any secrets when dealing with his confessor, his doctor or his lawyer.

* * * * *

The following incident, arising in a *surprise* situation of this kind, found the embarrassed defense attorney meeting the situation with a sense of humor and perhaps more complacence than most lawyers could muster under similar circumstances: A railroad attorney, appearing in defense of an employee's negligence action in Supreme Court, was taken by surprise when one of his

74

own witnesses testified that he had noticed the hand brake was defective on a run-away freight car involved in the accident. When defense attorney hesitated, His Honor asked, "Have you any further questions of this witness, counselor?" whereupon the lawyer, with surprising but commendable candor, replied, "No, I think I'll quit while I'm behind."

* * * * *

Astute cross-examination is not necessarily the exclusive domain of the courtroom nor the undivided province of the lawyer, as witness the discomforting experience of a prominent urban attorney. His wife dropped by the office one day to be taken to lunch. On the way they passed a very attractive young lady who spoke pleasantly. Suspiciously, wifey asked, "Who's that?" and he said, "That's a girl I met professionally." Her rather poignant inquiry then was: "Whose profession, darling, yours or hers?"

* * * * *

Sometimes the answers you get from a witness are just plain confusing:
Q. "Did he ever get out of your sight?"
A. "No, I don't believe so."

Q. "He remained constantly in your sight?"
A. "I wasn't watching him constantly, but there wasn't any time that I looked at him that I didn't see him."

It is not always the lawyer who is confounded by the witness's answer. Sometimes it's the witness who is confused by the attorney's question: For example:

Q. "If this boy had been riding his bicycle in the street, down the middle of the street, just prior to the time of the collision, and turned to the right in front of you, would you believe that you would have seen him had he been in the street?"

Another one:

Q. "Is there any way, medically speaking, doctor, in which you can differentiate the amount of tension and complaint of pain to the emotional overlay as against those things which were actually present?"

Also:

Q. "If you signal to turn right but then turn-to-the-left-and-in-front-of then the other fellow is left no choice but to drive right between you, right?"

And:

Q. "Describe in your own words what happened."
A. When the ladder slipped on the stage I clutched the top rung, causing my feet to swing out as I fell, landing on the proscenium where I lay prostitute for some time."

*   *   *   *   *

Although definitely frowned on, under a strict code of ethics, and quite properly so, lawyers will sometimes risk on cross-examination the rage of opposing counsel and reprimand from the bench for a "shot in the dark" question in order to put across a point with a jury, knowing full well that the question will be ordered stricken and the jury instructed to disregard it. Typical is the following question, asked in "a wee hours of the morning" automobile collision case, where the lawyer for the defendant had reasonable cause to believe that the plaintiff had been out on the town and was somewhat "under the influence" at the time of accident, although the lawyer was unable to prove it:

Q. "Where did you obtain the bottle of whiskey that you had stashed in the glove compartment of your car?*

Of course this, quite properly, drew immediate objection and strenuous protestations from opposing counsel as well as reprimand from the bench, but the jury had heard, and who knows to what extent they might give credence to the implication in reaching a verdict.

This sort of thing is what is sometimes referred to in legal circles as a "HAVE YOU STOPPED BEATING YOUR WIFE" type of question.

* * * * *

One of the most opprobrious devices of the legislative process, in the enactment of bills into law, is the giving of "blank check" authority and power to administrative agencies to promulgate and publish rules, codes and regulations that shall have "the force and effect of law." Both Congress and the legislatures of the various states are guilty of this disingenuous practice.

The place for regulations that are penal in character, it would seem, is in the law itself, with opportunity to those affected to be heard with regard thereto, and not in a multiplicity of confusing and often contradictory codes, rules and regulations put out by the particular agency cloaked with responsibility for administration of the law.

Under this legislative scheme of doing things, the proprietor of the establishment that may be the target, or his representative, usually finds out about it for the first time when some inspector comes on the property and serves an order, listing the things he has failed to do or specifying the matters he must comply with. Usually, failure to comply within x number of days carries with it a penalty of x number of dollars for each day's violation or jail, or

* A question obviously subject to objection under rules of evidence if for no other reason as blatantly "assuming a state of facts not proven."

77

both, pursuant, as it were, to "Section XYZ, paragraph 13, subdivision 45 of Code rules, dated . . . " etc.

It should be noted that this is a "rule or regulation" carrying a penalty and drafted not by our well paid legislators but conceivably by some obscure individual or group in the particular administrative agency involved.

The stringency of most of these onerous regulations leads to the suspicion that the authors thereof could not care less whether these burdensome requirements do violence to the lawful rights of others.

This legislative practice would not be so bad if many of the things required to be done were reasonable and capable of compliance, at least within the time allowed.

A few years ago all of the railroads in a particular state were served with notice, under the usual threat of fines and penalties, by an administrative agency that they must provide "hot and cold running water" by a certain date in crossing watchmen's shanties. In many locations water would have to be piped great distances. In some places the pipes would have to be carried under the tracks. The type of water tank and heater specified led to speculation as to whether, after installation in the tiny shanty, there would be any room left for the watchman, if his physical proportions exceeded those of a Singer's Midget. This is only one example from a multiplicity of arbitrary and capricious orders issued at about the same time, many of them virtually incapable of reasonable compliance. The orders came so thick and fast that there was hardly time to digest their requirements before being in default.

Upon application by all of the railroads involved for a hearing on these orders, the state agency responsible apparently thought best to cancel or reasonably modify most of the orders rather than face appropriate court action.

* * * * *

"Lawyers' fees" may seem a strange subject for a book entitled "Legalaffs." There is nothing very funny abut a bill for legal services.

However, there is so much misconception and lack of understanding about this matter that a word or two on the subject of fees for legal services might not be amiss.

Probably the most prevalent complaint arises out of a situation where a client calls seeking immediate legal advice on a particularly pressing matter. The discussion may take an hour or two.

When the client receives a bill for this professional advice, he may scream bloody murder. "Why, he only gave me some verbal advice right off the top of his head—no instruments drafted, no court appearances—this is an outrage!" he cries.

Granting that there are instances of overcharging in all professions, this fact should be kept in mind. Many laymen are under the misconception that when a person graduates from law school and passes his bar examination and is admitted to the practice of law, he's forever qualified without further research or study to advise a client, draft or probate a will, prepare a deed, foreclose a mortgage and sue or defend a law suit. This is not entirely the fact. Actually the newly admitted lawyer is just beginning the study of law. Like all practitioners he must keep up on the law if he hopes to maintain a successful practice and make a living as an attorney at law. Federal and state legislation is an ever-changing process, repealing and amending old laws and passing new ones. Courts likewise, with changing times and new legal concepts, are constantly overruling, modifying and interpreting the laws in a manner that can change the law so drastically that what you might advise a client last week could be disastrous this week.

This brings us to the crux of the matter of "lawyers' fees." It costs a lawyer a tremendous amount of time and money to keep abreast of these things. The cost of law books today is unbelievable. Purchase of even the basic volumes makes an awesome dent in a lawyer's exchequer, such as decisions of the United States Supreme Court, the lower federal courts and appropriate state court decisions. Books covering federal and state statutes must not only be purchased but kept up to date. They can become untrustworthy without expensive subscriptions to supplemental services to keep one abreast of changes, additions and amendments. Text books covering certain subjects and various digests are also essential.

When you see rows and rows of books on shelves in a lawyer's office, did you ever stop to ask yourself, "I wonder what those cost him?" It would curl your hair to know, and keeping what you see up to date is a never-ending process. A lawyer can't carry all the law in his head, but he has to know how and where to find it. If he doesn't have the tools he's dead. And tools cost money. Free advice and curbstone opinions are worth only what you pay for them.

* * * * *

V

POLICE COURT HUMOR

Police courts, for all their grim reality, are a prolific source of humor. Amazing and unique protestations of innocence, fractured syntax and mixed metaphor are never-ending sources of hilarity. To a marked degree, likewise are family, domestic and traffic courts. Over the years judges, lawyers, court reporters and others who knew that as a hobby I liked to keep a diary of such humorous "memorabilia" would from time to time send me a "dilly" or two, mostly from their personal experiences. Herewith are some of these, with appropriate "titles" I have taken the liberty to supply.

Solicitous Advocate

Prisoner charged with assault and battery. Plea by police court advocate: "Please, your honor, put my client on probation. That would be the mercenary [sic] thing to do."

Justice Notwithstanding

. . . and now, members of the jury, as you consider the preponderance of evidence pointing to the innocence of my client, just remember one thing—WE ARE HERE TO DISPENSE WITH JUSTICE."

Beyond Suspicion

Judge: "The charge is conducting 'Going Out of Business Sale' without the required city permit. How do you plead?"
Prisoner: "Not guilty, your honor. Our store is known as the 'UNSUSPECTED STORE OF SURPRISES.' "

Ouch

Defendant arraigned on charge of bigamy. He asked what the penalty would be if he pleaded guilty and His Honor said, "Two mothers-in-law."

Cagey Suburbanite

Prisoner examined by district attorney, seeking to show long prior criminal record:

Q. "Where were you on August 12 of last year?"

A. "I was living in the lovely village of Dannemora* while working for the state of New York."

In Extenso

Judge to prisoner complaining of "police brutality":

Q. "You say the arresting officer struck you with his club and injured your right arm?"

A. "That's right."

Q. "Can you raise your right arm now?"

A. "No."

Q. "How high could you raise it before he hit you?"

A. "Oh I could put it straight up like this" (illustrating).

Liquid Asset

Judge: "The charge is drunken driving and operating a defective motor car. How do you plead?"

Prisoner: "Not guilty. You have to be drunk to have the nerve to operate that car of mine."

Judge: "I'll drink to that. License revoked and $250.00 fine."

Fighting Hero

Judge to prisoner, charged with disorderly conduct: "Ever arrested before?"

* State prison.

82

A. "No, your honor, and I fought for three years in World War II for my country."

Judge: "Charge dismissed."

Pal to defendant on the way out: "Did you forget to tell the judge that it was the Italian army you fought in?"

Approved by Duncan Hines

Gaelic female charged with operating kitchen bar room in Boston. District attorney to defendant: "Do you fancy so many men going in and out of your kitichen?"

Defendant: "There were no fancy men in my kitchen."

Now Hear This

English magistrate to pub proprietor: "Why did you strike this sailor?"

Prisoner: "I hit him just once between the nose to get his attention. I always run a respectable 'ouse."

Busted Betrothal

Young couple arraigned on charge of masterminding floating crap game, asked by judge "Are you two married?" was told by gentleman prisoner, "No, yo honor, we were engaged but her mother broke up our brothel."

Real Pal

Pal of defendant asked by judge "What are you doing here?" answered, "He wants me to act as his interpolator."

Never on Sunday

Youthful defendant charged with simple assault—pinching lady from behind—said: "I plead not guilty, Your Honor, I thought it was my girl friend."

Over Matched

Old timer, charged with assault and battery, exclaimed on arraignment, "Assault and battery? Why I had all I could do to defend myself, she fought like a tiger."

Light Sentence

Irritated judge to very evasive prisoner charged with petit larceny: "I find you inscrutable."

Prisoner: "Oh, thank you, judge. I thought you were going to find me guilty."

Brush Off

Defendant charged with reckless driving and failure to yield to pedestrian. Complaining witness present, covered with dirt and mud. Judge to defendant:

Q. "Your occupation?"

A. "Chauffeur."

Q. "What's your explanation?"

A. "I was driving by and brushed him walking near the curb."

Q. "Brushed him—why, he looks like a chimney sweep. What kind of a car were you driving?"

A. "A city power street sweeper."

The Right Place

Lawyer to prospective juror: "Do you believe in capital punishment?"

A. "Oh sure, that's in Washington."

Alcoholic "Anomalous"

Prisoner to Judge: "But your honor, I've cut my drinking in half."

Judge: (caustically) "By eliminating all chasers, no doubt."

Seeing Red

Judge to brawler on arraignment: "Why did you hit the bartender?"

A. "He said I was comatose. I don't take that *Commy* stuff lying down."

Not Loaded

Judge: "Do you deny that you hit this man on the head with a bottle of gin?"

Prisoner: "Yes, Your Honor, it was an empty bottle. Besides, as he came at me I had to do something quick to disinclination [sic] him."

Mixed Metaphor

Judge to female Harlem character: "Do you deny that you operated a policy drop in your establishment?"

Prisoner: "Yes, Yo Honor, the only policy that ah mess around with is honesty is the best of."

No Linguist

Judge: "Is this testimony germane?"
Witness: "No, Your Honor, I only speak English."

Late Model

Police court magistrate: "The arresting officer's complaint states you were a driving inebriate."

Fuzzy Prisoner: "That's a lie, I was a driving a Chevy."

Righteous Indignation

Judge: "You are charged with creating a disturbance at the exchange desk of the Acme Department Store. What's your explanation?"

Defendant: "I brought back an electric toaster that wouldn't work. The trouble all started when this guy wouldn't give me a reprobate."

Power of Suggestion

Prisoner in San Francisco claiming alibi was having trouble remembering his whereabouts with respect to exact time and place. His harried attorney said: "Think hard now and try and orient yourself."

In jubilation, the prisoner cried: "That's it! I was in China Town, over Grant Avenue way."

Old Mexico

Judge: "Hold this prisoner incommunicado."

Prisoner: "You can't send me to Mexico until I see my lawyer."

No Place for a Lady

Complaining witness to night desk sergeant: "This guy deliberately trampled my trailing arbutus."

Sergeant: "Well, what was she doing in the garden at this time of night?"

Just Unlucky

Judge to old offender: Sometime I'll like to see you here when you're penitent."

Prisoner: "So would I, judge, but they only seem to bag me for being drunk and disorderly."

Dead Broke

Judge to confidence man: "Have you no scruples?"

Prisoner: "Not a sou, your honor; I can't even raise bail."

"Bonnie and Clyde"

Judge: "What's the prisoner's version of this incident, officer?"
Officer: "He claims he was standing on the corner of the alley, minding his own business, when this old lady came along, hit him over the head with her purse and stole his knife."

Sharp Customer

United States Attorney to prosecution witness in counterfeit case: "Did you realize that this bill was spurious?"
Witness: "No, but I could see right away it was a fake."

Sorry about That

Judge: "What's the charge against this man, officer?"
Officer: "Drunken driving, your honor."
Wife: (from rear of courtroom) "How come they only pick on him when he's been drinking?"

Old Pals

Judge: (to old timer charged with disorderly conduct) "Why do you want a week's adjournment, Heubert?"
Prisoner: "I want my friends here, judge, to hear you call me by my first name."

Fast Start

Judge: "Why did you sock the panhandler?"
Prisoner: "Somebody has to get this *War on Poverty* rolling."

Constitutional Rights

Arresting plainclothesman to well-known pickpocket: "What were you up to with your hand in my pocket?"

Prisoner: "What business is that of yours?"

Unacceptable

As prisoner was being led away, after pleading guilty to a reduced charge of murder, second degree, and given the mandatory (Massachusetts) sentence of life imprisonment, a lady acquaintance in front bench had this advice: "Don't serve dat sentence."

Prisoner's momentary look of hope faded to one of resignation with her further advice of "kill yo self," he obviously preferring to serve out the duration.

Self Preservation

Judge to lady complainant in assault case: "Why did you leap from his car so abruptly?"

Lady complainant: "For goodness sake."

The Hard Way

After interview with his attorney in his cell, prisoner anxiously asked, "Do you think I have a chance of beating this rap?"

His lawyer said, "Yes, break out tonight or hang yourself."

The Further the Better

Judge: "I'll suspend sentence if you'll get out of town."

Prisoner: "How far do you want me to go?"

Judge: "Have you got a car?"

Just Goofing Off

Three brawlers charged with felonious assault on grill patron. Judge: "The arresting officer says that when he arrived you were giving complainant a good working over."

First Prisoner: "Naw, we were just kidding around."

Judge: "Very well, let's see if the grand jury regards this as just friendly group therapy."

Just Testing

Couple arrested in grill disturbance after wild night on the town. Lawyer (to female client): "And when he got fresh you slapped his face?"

Client: "No, I thought he was dead."

Reckless Extravagance

Las Vegas character in court for non-payment of gambling debt. Judge: "What's your explanation for not paying what you owe?"

Gambler: "My wife blew the money on food and shoes for the kids."

Oh to Be Seventy Again

Judge to Old Sport: "Do you deny that you were chasing girls in the park?"

Old Sport: "I certainly do. With my gout I couldn't catch one downhill with the wind at my back. Morever, if I caught one I don't think I could remember what I chased her for."

No Stone Unturned

District attorney: "What effort did you make to apprehend the defendant's accomplice?"

Officer O'Flaherty: "Sure and we searched every crook and cranny."

Ivy Leaguer

Defendant arrested on complaint of female companion.

Judge: "What were you up to when seen walking through the park with the complainant on one arm and a blanket on the other?"

Defendant: "We were on our way to the Yale-Harvard football game."

Judge: "Oh."

Amateur Brain Surgeon

Judge: "Do you wish the court to appoint an attorney for you?"

Defendant: "Who needs one? I'm going to act as my own lawyer."

Judge: "Very well, and I hope you don't end up with an idiot for a client."

Bad Breath Commercial

Bunch of winos arrested and interrogated in line-up for "Rolling" drunk. Wino, protesting T.V. coverage of proceedings: "I object—we're on the air."

Police court magistrate: "Me too, I have to breathe it."

Amnesia Victim

Police court magistrate addressing confused drunk, victim of office party! "You say your wife won't let you in the house——?"

Woman complainant (interrupting): "Listen, judge, I never saw this guy before in my life until he rang our bell, cried, begged my forgiveness and then tried to push his way into our house."

For Better or For Worse

Judge: "You admit you've been drunk and disorderly for three days. Why?"
Prisoner: "My wife left me."
Judge: "Discouraged, eh?"
Prisoner: "No, celebrating."

Sink or Swim

Judge: "The officer says that he saw you attempt to push your wife out of the boat. What's your explanation?"
Prisoner: "I was trying to drown my sorrow."

A Bonus

Plaintiff: "I demand an immediate annulment."
Judge: "On what grounds?"
Plaintiff: "She said 'marry me and you get the best cook in town.' "
Judge: "Well, what's your beef?"
Plaintiff: "She didn't tell me the cook was her mother."

Intermezzo

Judge: "What's the domestic problem here?"
Wife: "All that he wants to do is watch football on television."
Husband: "That's not so. I always try to talk to her during the commercials."

For An Emergency

Referee in bankruptcy: "You appear to have an impressive list of liabilities, including hospital, doctor and dentist bills, grocery bills, default on mortgage and personal loans, to mention a few. Have you no assets?"

Bankrupt: "I've got about $5,000 in the bank, but I'm saving that for a rainy day."

Pleading "The Fifth"

Judge: "How do you plead?"
Prisoner: "I plead the fifth commandment."

Guidance Counselor

Judge to teen-age trouble-maker: "The officer says you're in trouble because of the group you hang out with. Who are they?"
T.A.T.: "My folks!"

Extrovert

Judge to bank official: "Are you able to identify the defendant as the man who stuck up your bank last Friday?"
Bank Official: "Yes, he came back in response to our ad that his pictures were ready. He said he'd like a set of prints for his mother."

Rock and Roller

Judge to long-haired creep lugging guitar: "What's your excuse for creating a disturbance at the Internal Revenue Office?"
Prisoner: "I was protesting my income tax."

Magna cum Laude

Judge: "Why did you hand the bank teller a stick-up note in Latin?"
Prisoner: "I wanted him to know that I was no ordinary stupid jerk."

You All Git Out

Judge: "Why were you quarreling with your neighbors?"
Defendant: "We came over to see their home movies. That was O.K., but they didn't have to play the *Star Spangled Banner* at the end."

Apprentice Jerk

Judge: (to juvenile delinquent) "Why did you strike your teacher?"
A. "I'm from a broken home. I have no parents to hit."

Dealer's Choice

Judge to automobile dealer: "Do I understand you recalled the defendant's car because of some defect?"
Plaintiff: "Yes, not in the car, in his bank account."

Retrogressive Female

Excited insured motorist 'phoned insurance company lawyer and said: "My wife just backed our car out of the garage."
Attorney: "What's so wrong with that?"
Client: "It was pretty frightening—I backed it in last night!"

Undismayed by the Futility of Endeavor

Judge: "Why were you picketing the United Nations Building with a blank sign?"
Prisoner: "I couldn't find a sponsor."

Stout Fella Just a Ghost

London (Reuters): "Handyman George Tucker told a court today that he drank more than 40 bottles of stout in a bar one evening, but was quite sober and could identify the man who stole his wallet."

Judge John Maude told him: "Surely you must be dead. It must be your ghost we are looking at."

In the Interest of Justice

Judge: "We're going to give you the sobriety test."
Prisoner: "That's O.K., Your Honor, but can I have about three hours to brush up for it?"

Cook Out

"What's your excuse for throwing garbage out of your second story window?"
Prisoner: "We were just getting ready for a *garbecue*."

Somniferous Justice

Judge, in long-winded address to jury, noticed juror number 7 sound asleep. Annoyed, His Honor said to juror number 6, "Would you mind waking that fellow up?" to which juror number 6 replied, "You wake him up, Your Honor, you put him to sleep."

Old Pro

Judge: "What makes you so sure your wife plans to remarry for the fifth time?"
Husband: "Because she's got that handy old wash-and-wear bridal outfit of hers drip drying in our bathroom."

Night Court Magistrate's Lament

I can't stand drunks, so gross, verbose,
　　Jokers who laugh at their own jocose,

Crying jags, sniveling, morose,
  I chicken out on the belicose,
    But I drink to those that are comatose.

—adk

Character Witness

He's a friend you can always lean upon,
  A virtual walking paragon,
  A gentleman always, this *John*,
    He's never socked a dame with his hat on.

—adk

Choosy Mendicant

Judge to street beggar faking crippled leg: "I'd go light on you except that next week you would probably be back feigning blindness."

Prisoner: "Not a chance, Your Honor. I tried that and found there were a lot of dishonest people tossing me slugs and lead nickles."

No Backbone

Judge: "The officer says you were drunk at the New Year's Eve party, created a disturbance and collapsed on the dance floor. What's your version of this?"

Defendant: "I wasn't drunk. I wore a turtle neck sweater with my tuxedo. That was a mistake. I always need a stiff, starched shirt to hold me up."

Judge: "I think a net under you would probably be more practical."

Home Work

Judge (to defendant charged with violation of the Federal Fair

Trades Act): "Pray how can you claim to be able to legally cut prices below those of your competitors?"

Prisoner: "I fool around with the books at night."

It's Dark in There

Drunk arrested for annoying the wild animals at a circus exhibit.

Judge: "Drunk or sober I would think you would know better than to stick your head in a lion's mouth."

Prisoner: "I know it's dangerous, but my father was a lion trainer and whenever I see a lion I can't resist looking for Dad."

Respect for Old Age

Judge to old timer: "What's your excuse this time for public intoxication?"

Prisoner: "It was like this, Your Honor. I fainted on the street and a crowd gathered. Someone said 'give him water.' An old lady said 'no, give him whiskey.' I was about to drink the water when someone else said, 'Why don't you listen to the nice old lady?' so I switched so as not to offend her and here I am."

The Winner

Judge: "Do you deny that you had to be carried out of the Golden Slipper night club?"

Prisoner: "Yes, Your Honor. I could have walked, but I enjoyed the honor of being carried."

Pushcart Diplomacy

New York East Side pushcart vendor arrested for doing business without a license. Judge: "I'll give you your choice, $50.00 fine or ten days in jail."

Prisoner: "Would you like to surprise me with a suspended sentence for good behavior or something?"

Malace Aforethought

Husband, a chemist, was indicted for systematically poisoning his wife with a drug concoction of his own composition. The district attorney, in handing up the indictment to the court, remarked "I suppose this might be properly designated as a case of *premedicated* murder."

Income Tax Dilemma

Male tax-payer to income tax examiner: "Can I take my brother-in-law as a deduction, he lives with us?"

Examiner: "No, but you can put him out."

Tax payer: "Oh, I can't do that because then my wife would leave and I'd lose her exemption."

Brotherly Love

Judge: "What's the charge against this man, officer?"

Officer: "He was picketing the Marine Recruting Station with a sign that said 'LOVE AND PEACE.' I said, 'How would you like to go in and sign up?' and with that he gave me a shove and said, 'How would you like a good punch in the snoot?' "

Lost and Found Department

Desk Sergeant: "What's your trouble, sir?"

Citizen: "Where's the officer who rescued my boy when he fell through the ice on the river?"

Desk sergeant: "Oh, he's changing his clothes."

Citizen: "Ask him what he did with the kid's hat."

A Familiar Face

Lady bank teller, suspected as an accomplice of a forger because of the large number of checks she had cashed for him, was asked by district attorney why she kept cashing his checks, and she said, "He had such a kind face and seemed to be such a good customer."

Help!!!

Thinking of unnecessary and frivolous procedures which burden the courts at times, a Supreme Court Justice in the state of Massachusetts once told of an active and flamboyant criminal practitioner who put on quite a show while "performing" in Superior Court and then took the matter up to the Supreme Court on exceptions. When he got there he told the justice that his client's rights really had not been violated in the Superior Court, but he thought the Supreme Court just might be able to think of something that they might be able to do to help his client out.

Velly Solly

A young Chinese American was testifying in court in Boston one day and it seemed plain that he was making like "Mickey the Dunce." He probably understood English better than he did Chinese. They had an interpreter there who was cutting himself in for a few bucks and doing the best he could. The district attorney asked the witness a question, and the witness, forgetting himself and not waiting for the interpreter to do his stuff, replied in *English*. The interpreter nevertheless (perhaps with his fee in mind) then turned to the jury and gave them the answer again in his best Cantonese dialect.

Synchronizing Watches

Magistrate: "Were you ever up before me?"
Prisoner: "I'm not sure, judge. What time do you get up?"

Didn't Know It Was Loaded

Female defendant living with victim of homicide without benefit of clergy, after learning he had been dallying with another dilly, took over-sized shotgun and pulled the trigger, nearly blowing him in halves. When asked by the Court if she had anything to say on disposition, she replied, "Yo Honor jedge, ah didn't mean to kill him."

Can't Tell the Players Without a Program

Defendant accused of knocking down lady passenger in rush for seat in London underground train.

Magistrate, in dismissing complaint with lecture: "I suggest in the future you watch your manners better. Try to be somewhat more of a Sir Galahad. Next case."

Defendant, returning to courtroom and interrupting proceedings: "Excuse me, my lord, but what was the name of that titled gentleman again?"

He Made a Hit with the Law

Houston (UPI)—A small well-dressed but nervous man was led into the lineup room at police headquarters Monday. He fidgeted under the bright lights when an officer asked him what he had been arrested for.

"I hit my mother-in-law," he replied.

"Release that man," cried someone from the darkened audience.

"Give him a medal," another shouted.

The officers and victims in the room gave the suspect a standing ovation.

Nice Try

Weston, W. Va. (UPI)—Danny Beverlin, 19, was rifling a patrolman's locker in the back of the city jail Monday when police barged in on him.

Feigning amnesia, Beverlin moaned, "Where am I?"

An officer shoved him into a cell and replied, "You're in jail."

Involuntary Postponement

Judge to bank embezzler: "Sorry to interrupt your planned vacation in South America. I suggest you make no reservations before 1978."

Keep Walking

Prisoner 'phoned his lawyer and excitedly said, "They have shaved my head and split my pants leg, what do I do now?"
His lawyer advised, "Don't sit down."

Wedded Bliss

Police court magistrate to night club dancer, arrested for insufficient attire, asked, "Are you married?"
She said, "No, but I'm engaged."
Magistrate: "When are the nuptials?"
Dancer: "There will be no nuptials until we are married."

Premature

Judge: "The charge is attempted arson at your store last night——"
Prisoner (interrupting): "Not last night, tomorrow night."

Solving the Garbage Disposal Problem

Judge: "What's the charge against this man?"
Officer: "Stealing a gift-wrapped package from the rear seat of an automobile."
Judge: "What was in the package?"
Officer: "Garbage."

Within Staggering Distance

Police court magistrate (to old offender): "How come, Red-

ford, you manage to find your way back here so often?"
Prisoner: "It's the shortest distance between two pints."

Impeccably Attired

Judge (to lady bank teller): "Do you recognize the prisoner as the person who robbed your bank?"
Teller: "I sure do. He stuck up our bank three times."
Judge: "Did you notice anything special about him?"
Teller: "Yes, he seemed to be better dressed each time."

Lead Foot

Judge to police officer: "When you were being chased in your prowl car by this gang of criminals at fifty-five miles an hour what did you do?"
Officer: "Seventy."

Hospitable Jurist

Judge: "Patrick O'Malley you are here for drinking."
Prisoner: "Well, what are we waiting for, Your Honor, let's get started."

Just Love and Peace

Judge, to hippy leader, arrested in connection with protest march: "This violent, irresponsible street demonstrating is inexcusable and will not be tolerated."
Hippy defendant: "But your honor, there was very little violence. One man was chocked but he escaped successfully."

* * * * *

Unfair to Organized Gambling

Judge, to gambler arrested for failure to have "gambler's

internal revenue stamp": "What do you mean you can win at cards but have no luck with the ponies?"

Gambler: "They won't let me shuffle the horses."

* * * * *

Strictly Personal

A "kissing bandit" was finally nabbed by the law. He made a practice of grabbing attractive women on the street, in elevators and other public places and kissing them passionately.

At his trial a woman complainant, although directed by the court to tell the jury what if anything the prisoner said while kissing her, refused because she said it was "too embarrassing." She did agree, however, to write it on a piece of paper.

What she wrote said, "I'm going to kiss you until the steam comes out your ears, honey." The note was passed from juror to juror. Juror number 11, a shapely dame, read it, then nudged male juror number 12, who was dozing, and handed him the note. He read it, looked the lady over approvingly and put it in his pocket. The judge said, "You will kindly hand the note to the bailiff."

"I certainly will not, Your Honor," said the juror firmly. "It's a personal matter."

Self-Control

Judge to prisoner: "The charge is public intoxication. The officer says you passed out and fell flat on your face on the barroom floor. What's your explanation?"

Prisoner: "I'll say this, Your Honor. I was the only one in the place that knew when to quit."

* * * * *

Double Jeopardy

Judge to pisoner: "Your explanation has severely strained my credulity."

102

Prisoner: "Oh boy, they bring me in for lifting a guy's wallet and now I'm being charged with giving the judge a hernia or something."

VI

FAMILY AND DOMESTIC RELATIONS COURTS

Connubial Bliss

Raffish character, charged with non-support by wife.

Judge: "What's your explanation for not performing your marital duty of support?"

Defendant: "Well, I always heard how tough it was to make a go of marriage if both parties worked, so I gave up my job. But I'll say this, I always help her up to get down to work on time."

Act of Congress

Judge, to wife complaining of husband's shenanigans: "What is there about your husband's behavior that you regard as incongruous?"

Wife: "Congress can't help this guy. He just drinks and he hates politicians."

Philharmonic

Family Court Judge: "You should try more conciliatory overtures to your wife."

Husband: "Are you kidding? I can't play a note and she hates music."

Odd Ball

Family Court Judge: "If you were not so querulous, madam, I think you and your husband would get along much better."

JUSTICE

NON OBSTANTE

LEGALAFFS

Wife: "You've got it all wrong, Judge. He's the queer one, not me."

Cat's Meow

Family Court Judge (to wrangling couple): "The wife should be the catalyst of the family."

Husband: "I'll drink to that. You won't find a cattier dame anywhere."

What's Your Excuse?

Family Court Judge: "Your wife says that you hang out in bars to all hours. Why?"

Errant husband: "All the bartenders that I know are lonely."

Lazy Bones

Family Court Judge: "It seems to me, sir, that your lack of proper affection towards your spouse may be the basis for all this marital discontent."

Wife: "You can say that again. He hasn't had a gleam in his eye since we had a short in our electric blanket about five years ago."

Calling Medicare

Family Court Judge (to poor provider): "What's the matter, don't you like work?"

Husband: "I lost my job on account of illness."

Wife: "Yeh, the boss got sick of him."

Gracious Living

Family Court Judge: "I don't understand, madam, what you have to complain about, with a wealthy husband and homes in New York, Florida and Puerto Rico."

Wife: "Yeh, but he only comes home to see me and the kids once a year in our East Side slum."

Trick or Treat

Family Court Judge: "What were you two fighting about this time?"

Husband: "She kept nagging me for money for a permanent and I said 'leave your hair as it is and I'll take you some place Halloween.' That's when the trouble started."

Christmas Spirit

Family Court Judge: "This is a time of peace. How come you two are quarreling when you should have the spirit of Christmas?"

Husband: "I tried, Your Honor. She said, 'What are you giving me for Christmas' and I said, 'How about an electric broom for the witch who has everything?' "

Affluent

Family Court Judge: "Your wife says that at the time she married you she thought you were well off."

Husband: "Guess I was; too bad I didn't know it."

Hi, Matey

Family Court Judge (to wrangling couple): "The charge is creating a disturbance at the Joneses' cocktail party. What's this all about?"

Wife: "I'm sick and tired of him introducing me at parties as his LITTLE ROOMMATE."

Two Car Family

Family Court Judge: "What were you two fighting about this time?"

Wife: "Well, I accidentally crumpled a fender on the family car and I said, 'If I had my own car you would not have to worry about it' and he said, 'O.K., I'll get you a tow truck.' "

Despicable Character

Family Court Judge (to husband): "You should be more amenable around the house."
Wife: "Oh come on, judge, he's about as meanable as they come right now."

Hobbies

Lawyer: Q. "Now tell me this. While you were still living with your wife, did she have any hobbies?"
A. "What do you mean hobbies?"
Q. "You know, hobbies. Like did she plays card or run around with other men?"

Early Riser

Family Court Judge: "What's so wrong with a wife awaking a husband with an alarm clock at 7:00 A.M.?"
Husband: "What, by throwing it at him?"

Maintaining the Status Quo

Family Court Judge: "If you can't get along with your husband why don't you give him a divorce?"
Wife: "What, and make the bum happy after all my years of misery?"

Considerate Spouse

Family Court Judge (addressing wife of wrangling couple): "It looks as though you woke up grumpy this morning?"
Wife: "No, I let the jerk sleep."

Question of Intestinal Fortitude

Family Court Judge (to wife complaining that her husband is allergic to labor): "He looks healthy enough. Does he have any physical defects?"

Wife: "Yeh, no stomach—for work, that is."

Judicial Sagacity

Family Court Judge (to husband complaining of wife's perfidy): "Whether a man winds up with a nest egg or a goose egg depends on the chick he marries."

Perfectionist

Family Court Judge (to angry wife): "What's so wrong with a husband being a perfectionist?"

Wife: "He's impossible around the house. Would you believe it, he insists that I brush even my dentures vertically."

TRAFFIC COURT ANECDOTES

Gutsy Driver

Judge: "The charge is failure to keep to the right. How do you plead?"

Prisoner: "Not guilty, Your Honor. The sign said, 'DON'T CROSS LINE IF YELLOW.' That's a challenge that no red-blooded American boy can resist."

Poor Mileage

Judge: "Mrs. Smythe, this is your second appearance in Traffic Court this month. What happened this time?"

Mrs. Smythe: "Sorry, judge, but I pushed down hard on the accelerator instead of the brake."

Judge: "I think I should remind you, Mrs. Smythe, that you are now averaging only about twelve miles to a fender."

Helpful Spouse

Judge: "Mr. Jason, you are charged with driving through a red traffic light——"

Mrs. Jason (interrupting from rear of courtroom): "Excuse me, Your Honor, but don't you give any consideration to the fact that this is the first time he's ever been caught?"

Good Connections

Judge: "Officer, why did you arrest this motorist?"

Officer: "I said, 'Your license calls for glasses.' "

Judge: "Well..."

Officer: "Then he said 'I have contacts.' "
Judge: "Lenses or politicians?"

Fringe Benefit

Judge (to persistent violator): "Tell me just one good thing about your driving."
Defendant: "It stopped my wife from bragging about me."

Back on His Feet Again

Judge (to driver of taxi, up for traffic violation): "How long have you been driving?"
Cabby: "Three days, Your Honor."
Judge: "How many accidents have you had?"
Cabby: "Three."
Judge: "Better try something else."
Cabby: "Like what, judge?"
Judge: "Like walking."

Hand Out

Judge (to local pastor): "Do you deny, father, that you failed to give a proper signal on making a left turn?"
Pastor: "No, but I'll say this, that's the first time in a long while that I didn't have my hand out."

Lots of Luck

Judge: "Don't you know, madam, that you turn-to-the-left-and-in-front-of at your own risk?"
Lady motorist: "But, Your Honor, I stuck my hand out and I had my fingers crossed."

Wrong Way Corrigan

Judge (to drunk driver): "What did you think you were doing, going the wrong way on a one-way street?"

Accused: "I don't know. Guess I was late, everybody seemed to be coming back."

Excuses Offered in Litigated Cases

(a) "To avoid a collision, I ran into the other car."

(b) "I collided with a stationary bus that was coming the other way."

(c) "My car had to turn sharper than was necessary owing to an invisible truck in the way."

(d) "I blew my horn, but it didn't work because it had been stolen."

(e) "I misjudged a lady crossing the street."

(f) "Coming home I drove into the wrong house and collided with a tree I didn't have."

(g) "I told the other idiot what he was, and went on."

Positive Identification

Lawyer: "Do you claim that you were struck by an automobile operated by my client?"

Victim: "Yes."

Lawyer: "Did you get the license number?"

Victim: "No, but I'd recognize that laugh anywhere."

One to a Customer

Judge: "How many traffic summonses have you issued to Mrs. Williams this week?"

Officer: "Three, your honor."

Judge: "Better give her one of our season tickets on her way out."

Traffic Court's Sage Advice

We are told to watch out for the other guy,
all rules of the road he'll defy,

So never this fool his tenets pursue
  lest that "other guy" turn out to be you.
        —adk